# The Incredible True Story

By: Baruc Lara

ISBN: 9798675712823
ISBN-13: 9798675712823

# Contents

# DEDICATION

6

This book is dedicated to my parents who inspired me to live, to my family who taught me how to live and to my teacher who encouraged me to write my stories.

# SPONSORSHIPS

Individual Sponsors:

Mo Anderson

Robert Funk Jr.

Pattye Moore

Kirk Humphreys

Itza Lara

Steve Slawson

Jeff Dixon

# ACKNOWLEDGEMENTS

# FOREWORD

Co-Editor's note:

First of all, this isn't a normal book. If you were looking for a normal book with a normal story, you'll probably be disappointed. There's no normal story or normal plot – for good reason. This is a story about life. In real life, there's no manufactured plot. There are no fictional characters or surreal elements that make it sound like an anomaly of real life. Instead, this is a story about growth. It's a story about learning, and ultimately pursuing a life more dedicated to what's most important in each of our own lives. When Baruc asked me to edit one of the early drafts, I'll never forget something he told me: "I'm not telling you to listen to me, I'm only telling you to think."

There are elements of Christianity in the words, but in the editing of the book, Baruc wanted to emphasize that this isn't a "Christian" book. It's not a "Hispanic" book or a "white" book. It falls into no categories and has no target demographic. Baruc wanted this to be a book that can in some way, somehow, speak to all. I am a Christian, but it's been a while since I've been to church. My knowledge of Christ is far from being able to produce verse after verse from memory as Baruc so eloquently can. In fact, that's part of the reason why Baruc asked me to edit the book. My upbringing is different from his. My race is different from his. He didn't want this to be a book that speaks exclusively to those identical to himself – for good reason.

Oftentimes we grow so comfortable– so complacent – in where we are that we forget about what we *could* be. In today's age there are so many people who focus on our differences in an effort to divide us instead of focusing on what brings us together. At the end of the day we are one planet and one people. We have more in common that brings us together than what separates us apart. That's the meaning of all of our own incredible true stories. But there's something special about this book. With other books, when the last page is turned, the story is over. In this book, when the last page is turned, your story might only be beginning.


-Brayden Love

11

# INTRODUCTION: Why?

You might be wondering: why my story? Why am I writing my story and sharing it with you? Well, for starters, it's the journey my story has led me on that has made me who I am today. My story, my journey, and what it has taught me is what encouraged me to start my own scholarship as a senior in high school for students who want to obtain a higher education. It encouraged me to then start my own leadership nonprofit underprivileged communities across the state, and it pushed me to pursue a higher education and get involved as much as I can. It motivated me to become a public speaker and enabled me to spread messages encouraging individuals to start their own positive action to change the world. It gave me the dream to become a social entrepreneur in an effort to teach the next generation of entrepreneurs that profit isn't about selfishness, but it is about selflessness. It encouraged me to one day run for political office to reshape where I live and bring about a better future for generations to come. It pushed me to live a more responsible and purposeful life. But, most importantly, it encouraged me to share, and hopefully after you have read my story, it will encourage you to tell your story, because it is your story that will open the world to new possibilities.

But why storytelling – why is it so important? The answer is simple: life experiences. The world pushes a false narrative that age is a tell-all for knowledge. Society tells us that the old are experienced and the young are ignorant. Why does it matter if you're not old enough to know better? I'm a 20-year-old writing this, what good are my experiences, right? Before you hear my story, I want you to understand these things.

Storytelling, why do we do it? Well for starters, everyone does it. Storytelling is significant to life because it allows us to communicate ideas, thoughts, and emotions. We are created to live, to experience, and to learn. From what we do, we come to a better understanding of life. Different ideas are displayed, different ideas are challenged, and different ideas are published for everyone to see and learn. That's why telling your story is so significant to the world, because everyone's individual story is what keeps the world going, it is what unites the human family, it is what inspires, what motivates, what generates love, sorrow, sympathy, and types of emotions that are so incredibly necessary for a person's existence. Something that I love to say is that it doesn't matter who you are talking to – you can learn from everyone. The beauty of storytelling is the experience of the person; it's beautiful to see how a person is able to relate or present an emotion and through that emotion is able to connect with or inspire someone.

How a person finds their story is special. The measures and risks a person takes to experience things contributes vastly in the search for how to live life and its meaning. The actions a person takes in life, the passions of what that person likes to do, their life mission. How you find your story is so special in the sense of how you are always searching for a new adventure to tell, new lessons to learn, and a life worth living. But the coolest part is how you put the story together, to tell a story that has never been told before, ideas that have never been talked about, and perspectives never seen. How will you plan to tell that story?

There must be more to storytelling, right? Storytelling shows how authentic a person truly is, the essence of storytelling is to be vulnerable; vulnerability shows courage and a person's true self. The person's true self is what this world needs and that is how it shows the authenticity of a person. but I believe it also promotes connection, perspective, and understanding. Storytelling builds life differently for others to see. Essentially, your experiences matter. That is why your story is so unique: the world is baffled at times by their daily lives, they don't know that others live something far different, they don't know that in someone else's head, it's an entirely different world. Telling your story opens people up to a different world of culture, lifestyle, and teachings. And the best part of telling your story is that it's yours and no one can change it or add to it, it's yours to tell, so own it, embrace it, and live up to it, because it's your incredible true story.

From the outside, storytelling is more than sharing your life experiences, it allows you to examine your life in a way where you are to put your experiences in history. What do I mean by this? History is taken in a manner of displaying the events of humanity, the ideas shared, the sciences discovered, the religion created, and the events that changed us, but the beauty of history is to look at it and intellectually examine it, we must have discussions. Ask why? We need to ask how? We need to study the mannerism, the ideology of human existence and the acts of human nature. Once we study these things the byproduct of this is human outcomes. Our outcomes.

The Incredible True Story is a set of experiences displayed in my history, but it's less of telling a story and more of understanding and examining the history of my experiences and asking why, how, studying my mannerisms, my human nature, and the human ideology that I found. The purpose of this is to share the outcomes of my experiences, but the point is for you to see why I made these outcomes; more importantly, it is for you to see the questions I was proposed that directed me to these outcomes. Within the path of a human, we are in a psychological dilemma of comfort and chaos. To be comfortable in where we are or to explore a chaos of adventure and new experiences. Well we need a bit of both in life, we need comfort and order to direct us to our north star in life, but we also need chaos to build experiences too, that will give us the resilience and wisdom to direct us to our true north. The way we find this is by answering a set of thought provoking, time consuming, philosophical questions. Every person needs to ask themselves questions that provoke reflection, responsibility and purpose, through this we direct ourselves to our true north in life. Within my Incredible True Story, you will find within the chaos of the adventure, a comfort and order that I believe will allow us all to direct ourselves to our true north. Within my Incredible True Story, we find the three themes which are rooted within every human. We find reflection from your past, present and future. We then move to purpose. The three purposes rooted in all humans are gratitude, service and love. Lastly, responsibility, for reflection, purpose and freedom. Within my Incredible True Story, we will highlight these three themes.

So, this message is to you, the young people and to the rest of the world. To examine my life and to do the same for yours. To see if you are living in comfort and order or if you are living in too much chaos. To purposefully understand where you have been and where you are going. And, to find that where you are going you will need responsibility and purpose.

Now that we have set the standard, I hope you enjoy my incredible true story.

-Baruc Lara

# Chapter 1: Me, Myself, and I

*"Selfish-a judgement readily passed by those who have never tested their own power of sacrifice."*

*—George Eliot*

To begin, I was born in Los Angeles, California, but raised in the plains of Oklahoma. I am the son of Roberto and Ana Rosa Lara, a brother to Ramsel, Itza, Xcaret, Giovanni, Maximillion, and Fatima Lara. My family moved to Oklahoma when I was just a baby.

Growing up, I was fortunate enough to say I didn't struggle. My parents were always able to provide more than enough for my siblings and I had access to the schools, clothes, travel, cars, and anything I wanted or needed. As a young kid, I wasn't challenged to do anything with my life. There was no sense of direction or purpose. My dad worked hard and we were very wealthy. So much so, that up to a point, I took advantage of my dad's hard work and this privileged life he'd provided for me. It made me very rebellious growing up, it made me selfish, I wasn't considerate, or grateful. This is no shot to my parents, at times us young people think we have it handled, but we don't. As a kid, I wasn't sure who I was or what I was becoming. I was just being a kid, of course. That's what we all go through. I used to cause chaos all the time—in church, at school, and at home. I was a goofball who didn't care about anything because I thought I was going to be young forever. I was growing up to be a selfish, ungrateful person.

Growing up in Oklahoma, I lived in my own world. My parents did their best to help me realize that there was more out there for me, but like I said, we young people always think we have it figured out, but I didn't, and I was completely wrong not to listen to my parents. You know what they say, live and learn, and boy did I.

I named this chapter "Me, Myself, and I" because at a young age we tend to only think about ourselves. The formula to live an unhappy life is simple, be ungrateful, live without purpose and take responsibility for nothing. This story focuses on my development as a person, but it also focuses on how I learned. I believe storytelling holds an important element: self-awareness. I realized how incredible my story is when I began to be aware of what I had and what I experienced.

So, let me ask you these questions: Are you grateful for what you have? Are you content with life? How do you live your life every day? You may be saying, "but Baruc, I'm only this age, I don't know better," or "I haven't lived as much." To you, the reader, I say that you are writing your story every day, even if you don't realize it. Go out and make the day a beautiful adventure. When the day turns, that page is written. Make the best of what you do and always remember a story is told not by what you do but how you do it.

Before I tell you my incredible true story, you must hear my parents' incredible true story.

# Chapter 2: The Beginning

*"True education is a kind of never-ending story—a matter of continual beginnings, of habitual fresh starts, of persistent newness."*

—J.R.R. Tolkien

A poor boy was living in Mexico. He woke up every day, committed to helping his parents. He was the third sibling of the family and the first boy of a family of seven. Since he dropped out of school early, he had no future in education. His future seemed dark, as he appeared to be on a path of poverty for the rest of his life. In his mid-teens, his father walked out on him and his family; having become involved with another woman, he left. Now it was up to this young man to take up the male role in the family. One thing that set this young man apart was his drive and determination. He had a work ethic that no one could match, and he also had dreams. He dreamed that he would one day get married and have a big family of his own. He had the desire to travel the world. He might have a dark road ahead of him, but all he could see was light at the end.

There was a girl, a small baby girl, who had been born into a vibrant and wealthy family in Mexico. She was the youngest in her family of twelve. Born and raised in a good household, this young girl grew up with only one pain: She never really knew her mother. Her mother died when she was just a baby. Her father had become so wounded from what happened to his wife that he sent the young girl off to live with her older sister. Her father eventually got himself right and remarried, and at that time, the young girl came back to live with her father. She lived well. She attended school and went through her daily life, seeing her future as bright and healthy. There wasn't anything stopping her from achieving any of her goals. She had plans to travel and live a happy life. She was also daddy's little girl, given whatever she wanted. She lived a good life.

Throughout the young man's life, he witnessed many hardships. He would see his mother leave to go to work very early and not come home until the next night. He would see people get shot, he would have guns pointed at him, and he would see people abusing drugs. Through all of these struggles, the young man would always persevere, but there was an older man whom the young man respected, his next-door neighbor. The young man would do chores for him for a bit of extra money. He would clean his porch, carry bags, and do anything else the man asked him to do. The young man always respected his neighbor; you could say he even saw him as a role model. They kept up a good friendship through the years until the young man had to leave.

The young man and his family eventually moved to California. The young man's mother built up a great business there. It would be several years before the man ever returned home to Mexico. He longed for his childhood home, even though he knew he had a new life in California.

One warm evening, his mother gave him the news that he would be returning to Mexico to handle some business for her. The man was filled with joy, knowing he would be able to return to his land and see his people again. However, the young man did not realize that his life would see a drastic change during this trip.

He returned to his old home. He visited his family and spoke about his new life in California and the business his mother was making. His relatives were delighted to finally being able to see this boy and his family succeed in life. The young man was able to eat at his favorite restaurants back in Mexico, and he enjoyed the sweet and tasty authentic flavors of his favorite dishes. He drank authentic Mexican beer until his thirst was satisfied. He was enjoying himself.

One day he decided to visit the wealthy older man who still lived next door. That evening he went and knocked on the door, and the older man invited him into his home. They talked for hours and hours about life, the struggles and glories of their lives. At one point in the evening, a young woman walked down the stairs to introduce herself to the young man. It was as if the young man had just seen an angel. He was twenty-eight years old, and he had never seen anything like her before. He was at a loss for words. His hands began to sweat, and he started shaking. He thought to himself all the possibilities with this woman, their future together, how they could create a family and travel the world, and eventually how they could grow old together. He envisioned his whole life with her in the shortest time possible, but he then stood up to impress the young lady by firmly extending his hand. He said, "Hello, I'm Roberto Lara."

The young woman had lived most of her life watching her father. He was her hero, and she was never away from him. She got along with her stepmother just fine, but her connection with her father was the most substantial connection of her life. She would follow him and see him coach and play soccer, and she would tag along with him at work. She did everything for her father —- she even went to school to impress her father. All she had in her mind was to become successful and always make her father proud. Even though she was intelligent and beautiful, she didn't have many boyfriends. She was living a very blessed life, but one thing she always did was pray for her future husband. Even though she would tell many people that a man was not in her sight, she would still pray for her future husband, already loving him to the best of her ability. In her prayers, she would show her devotion to him, her love, and her tenderness. She expressed to God all of the qualities she needed to find in her future husband and explained how much she was willing to sacrifice for him. One evening, just a few months from graduating from law school, she was in her room studying and preparing herself for her final exams. She heard two men speaking downstairs. One was undoubtedly her father, but there was another voice that she couldn't put a name or face, but one that for some reason sounded so familiar to her. She went downstairs to see her father talking to a young man, and to her eyes, he was the most handsome man she had ever seen. She saw a tall and muscular man, at the sight of whom she suddenly became nervous. She didn't feel like she looked beautiful. She saw this man, and she quickly reflected on her prayers. Immediately she was hoping that he was the one she had been praying for, but at the same time she felt like a guy like him would never be interested in her. She saw him stand and extend his hand to greet her. When he said, "Hello, I'm Roberto Lara," the young woman nervously extended her hand. "Hi, Roberto. I am Ana Rosa."

The two young lovers introduced each other as they had just met for the first time, but they had known each other from their childhoods. Growing up as neighbors, they would see each other every other day, but never really acknowledged one another. They lived their lives far apart, not knowing that one day they would see each other again. Looking into each other's eyes, they started to realize that they were made for one another.

Roberto and Ana were two people who were brought together by the grace of God. Ana knew that Roberto was the man for whom she had prayed about for many years, and Roberto knew that Ana was the woman about whom he had daydreamed for so long: having a big family, traveling the world together, and growing old with her. When they shook hands and looked each other in the eye, it was the moment that signified the start of a new life.

Roberto continued to go to visit the older man, for that was his excuse to see Ana. He would see her daily, bringing her flowers, and they would spend hours talking and gazing into each other's eyes. They spent so much time together that Roberto one day finally mustered up the courage to ask her out on a date. Roberto knew from the start that Ana was his true love, and he knew that Ana was the woman with whom he wanted to spend the rest of his life. True love is patient, and Roberto had waited until he was twenty-eight years old to find the love of his life. Roberto knew the love he had for Ana was profound – it was revolutionary. He felt it in his soul, and he knew it would ultimately be the power responsible for transforming his life. It was at this moment Roberto knew then he was ready to love Ana forever, unconditionally, with undying love.

Ana enjoyed seeing Roberto every day. She enjoyed hearing his voice and watching him listen attentively as she spoke about her life. To Ana, being with Roberto felt natural – it felt right. Ana saw Roberto as the answer to her prayers for a husband. As she went through her daily life, being with Roberto just felt right. She felt an instant connection. That was all she had ever asked God for, a great man, so she believed that this must have been God's elaborate plan for her. She loved Roberto at first glance, and she felt more confident and happier by the day. She knew that no one could stop their love for each other from growing. She was ready for whatever they would face.

Roberto and Ana went out on several dates. They were on their way to a future together. Roberto realized that he would have to return to California soon, but the thought of leaving Ana was unbearable. He wanted to stay with her for the rest of his life.

Roberto knew he was ready for marriage and knew God would be there every step of the way. Ana and Roberto both believed their love was God's grand plan for them.

Roberto asked Ana on a date to visit the opera. Roberto told Ana to dress up and that it would be a magical night for them. Ana wore a beautiful white dress with jewelry shining bright, and she looked beautiful—beautiful on earth and in heaven. Roberto's tall, strong build paired with a handsome tuxedo made him look like quite the gentleman. They rode in a nice car and were welcomed into the opera by the lights and music. They shared an enchanted evening, but the real magic was yet to come.

The opera concluded and the couple took a stroll through a beautiful park close to the opera house. As they were engaged in conversation, Roberto turned to look into her eyes and dropped onto one knee, looking at her with confidence and peace in his heart. He knew it was meant to be and she was going to say yes to his sacred question. As Ana was looking down at him, her heart filled with emotion, and she spoke a yes that would echo through their lives forever. Her eyes, filled with love, sparkled in the moonlight. Her "yes" contained compassion, truth, and strength. Roberto and Ana's love was so different from how they believed the world portrayed love. Their passion was supernatural. It was a charitable love, a love that consisted of the ultimate sacrifice to one another. It was an act of their will, and their love came from the soul itself.

After their wedding, Roberto and Ana waited a few months for the green card process to be completed. Throughout this time, Ana was struggling. She came to the realization that she was married, and she would soon have to leave her family. Roberto lived in California, and they both knew that America would be a better place for their future. However, the idea of leaving her first love, her father, tortured her every day. She didn't eat much during that time. For the first time ever, she felt the decision she made might not have been the right one. Ana's relationship with her father was important to her. She loved him so much, and now she had to look into his eyes and say goodbye. She was heartbroken over the situation. Through it all, Roberto made sure he was there for her. He made sure she had the attention, warmth, and faith she needed. Little by little, Roberto started filling the holes in Ana's heart that had previously been filled by her father. It wasn't that Roberto was taking her father's spot in her life, but that Ana realized Roberto was the man who would become the father of her kids. Love consists of sacrifice, and she was willing to sacrifice and say goodbye to her family for Roberto. That's how powerful her love was for Roberto. Ana and Roberto had reached the end of the process to obtain a green card and were ready to start their adventures in America. Although it was far from easy, with Roberto's constant companionship and assurance, she was finally ready to start her new life.

The newlyweds made their way to California. They stayed in Roberto's mother's home, which she frequently rented out to people. It was a tiny home, but it was big enough for the two of them. Roberto was an up-and-coming mechanic and had taught himself how to fix small engine motors. He went out every day to work long, hard hours for the rent, but he enjoyed it. Being with Ana and beginning something new gave him a great feeling of happiness. Roberto had always been a hard worker, and he had the right mindset. Eventually, he saved enough money to open his own shop. The two were well on their way.

The days began going more slowly for Ana. She didn't work, and she was struggling to learn English. She became very lonely. Roberto worked all day long, while she was alone at home. She began to miss Mexico. She thought about her dad every day, and the sense of loneliness became increasingly difficult. Ana prayed daily and asked God to keep her secure for her marriage. She knew it would all work out because God protected her marriage—and it did work out. A few months later, a wonderful blessing came upon the family. Ana found out she was pregnant with her first child. Ana and Roberto were so happy to begin this new journey with a child.

In what felt like a blur, nine months passed and Ana's first child was born. They named him Ramsel. Ramsel provided a new outlook on life that gave Ana hope again. Ramsel became Ana's best friend. He was God's answer to Ana. She was no longer lonely because she now had company every day while she was waiting for Roberto to come home. All she needed was Ramsel. She enjoyed cleaning his diapers, she enjoyed bathing him, she enjoyed dressing him, she enjoyed loving him. Ana fell in love all over again. She fell in love with Ramsel as naturally as she had fallen for Roberto. Her love for her husband had never been stronger. After about a year, the family grew once more. To their delight, God had blessed them with another healthy baby boy, Itza. To his excitement, Ramsel had a partner in crime, and Ana and Roberto now had a purpose far more significant than just the love they felt for each other: They had a family.

Ana was no longer lonely, for she had the company of her two boys. She loved being with them, and she spoiled her boys. She bathed them with love, she built them up with attention, and she taught them about Christ. These two boys were her whole world. She grew close to them. When they cried, Ana would come to their rescue. When they laughed, it was because their mother had made a joke, and if they were sad, it was because they saw their mother in a state of mourning. Ana was those boys' very first love. Roberto, on the other hand, enjoyed his boys as well, but he was missing something. Roberto was missing another girl in his family. He had wanted to have a daughter whom he could love and care for.

A few years after Itza was born, they found out God had blessed them with another child. Roberto prayed constantly for a girl. He did good deeds so that God would give him a baby girl. He did everything possible to have good fortune for his future child. So, when Ana delivered her baby, Roberto was able to lay his eyes on his answer from God. Roberto leaped with joy because God had sent him his baby girl. When Roberto glanced at her, it was like he had fallen in love all over again. He held his princess in his arms and named her after the Mayan goddess Xcaret.

Roberto would wake up every night to change her diaper. He would bathe her, change her, feed her, hold her, love her, and do everything for her. He made sure he was always there for Xcaret — to be there when she had a nightmare, to be there when she fell and hurt herself, and to be there and hold her after a broken heart. Xcaret loved her father, and there would be days when she would not stop crying, but as soon as she heard her daddy's voice, she would calm right down. She would rest her arms on him and fall into his love, knowing that nothing would ever happen to her. Nothing else mattered when she was with her daddy, and nothing caught her attention but her father. Her love for him was powerful, and they were always together. Ana and Roberto's family had grown, and so did the passion the two felt for their children. Roberto had his girls, and Ana had her boys. At that point, they thought it was their moment. Ana and Roberto both decided to hold off on having any more children for a few years. They were happy with their family. The family had grown so fast, and they had to learn how to manage it all. Throughout this time, Ana and Roberto started realizing that California might not be the perfect place to raise a family. Roberto had many different ideas and ways to raise his family, but he saw none of those dreams being accomplished in California. This revelation caused the family to start thinking about various places to live. They thought about leaving Los Angeles and moving to an area like Big Bear, but it didn't really feel right. They were afraid that their children would not grow up being close with their family. In this situation, they feared that they would grow up alone. Ana and

Roberto knew the price they would pay if they left, but it was a price they were willing to pay. Their love was far greater than anything, and they knew the sacrifices they would have to make in order to provide their kids with the lives they wanted for them.

At some point in this process, they were told about Oklahoma. At first, they didn't pay it much attention, but they prayed about it. Through the days, they heard mentions of Oklahoma more and more. They saw it as God's sign to investigate further, so they made a trip to Oklahoma. They found a small state with seemingly endless plains. However, they also saw a place with untapped potential that was growing day by day. Even the biggest city, compared to California, was small and quiet. There was very little traffic, and it was filled with friendly people.   They went through the neighborhoods and saw happy children playing out on the street. Ana and Roberto thought it was crazy because in California it would be unthinkable for children to do such a thing. They saw the steadiness of the state. As they saw more and more of Oklahoma, they began to realize God had answered their prayers. The idea of a perfect place to raise a family in solitude with space to grow was coming to fruition right before their very eyes. They found the perfect place to raise their family.

Knowing what they had to do, they returned to California to prepare for their journey. When they broke the news to the rest of the family, the others were confused. They had thought that their parents were satisfied in California. However, as parents, Ana and Roberto viewed decision-making in a different way than the rest of their family did. They took everything into consideration, and they wanted to live in the best place for their children to succeed. They wanted the best place to teach their children how to be strong-minded and not easily influenced, and they wanted the right place to raise their children where they could show them how to act, talk, present themselves, and become strong and independent. Ana and Roberto understood that a child needs a delicate balance of attention, direction, and responsibility. They also realized that California was a place filled with different kinds of influences. It was a faster-paced lifestyle that posed different problems and distractions. The craziness of California was no longer suitable for the family's needs. Instead, Oklahoma, a small but growing state, would be the best place for their children could thrive.

Through all this process, they decided to grow their family with another child. This child was different. Ana had much trouble with this child. The child was larger in size – bigger by far than her previous children. During her pregnancy, she had difficulty standing up, and couldn't be up for long due to the child's astounding weight. There came a night during her ninth month when Ana prayed to God for the arrival of the baby. Crazy how God works—the baby arrived a few hours later. Ana felt much pain during her delivery, but all glory to God, she had a healthy boy. She named him Baruc, which is Hebrew for "blessed" or "good news."

Roberto and Ana loved their big family, and on their way to Oklahoma, they found out they were expecting yet another child. They felt so blessed with the news. Ana and Roberto had been so happy with everything that they had accomplished together.

They made it to Oklahoma and bought a house. They enjoyed all the free space, a luxury they couldn't enjoy in California. Ana would take her kids to walk every day and play with them outside. After the move, they enjoyed more family time together than they ever had before. This had been the plan for the couple, to move to a place like Oklahoma City and finally be able to call it home. Oklahoma was the place where they would raise their children and grow old together. For Ana and Roberto, this was true happiness.

They started to settle more into the community and found a doctor for their kids. During their checkups with the new doctor, they found something troubling with Ana. The doctor informed them that Ana had developed a condition that caused significant risk of death to the child in her womb. They decided to do further exams on her to see how accurate this diagnosis was. They waited nervously for days. Eventually, days turned into weeks, and the weeks turned into months. Throughout this time, they prayed to God, and they trusted in the Lord's will. They finally got a call from the doctor. The doctor broke the news, telling them that the tests have shown it was medically proven that Ana could not give birth to children. In the face of the awful news, Ana and Roberto were calm. They didn't cry or go crazy at the news. They continued with their regular routine and decided to go through with having the child despite hearing the news. They had four children already, so what was stopping them now?

To the amazement of the doctor, Ana went into labor a few months later. While the doctor continued to marvel at Ana's "miraculous" progress. Roberto, on the other hand, was in the waiting room, praying and relaxed. The doctor came to him, asking why he wasn't worried that his child might die and that Ana could be in critical condition after a failed delivery. Roberto calmly responded that he had four children at home who were healthy and sound, so he saw no reason to worry this time. The doctor could not believe it; he was in complete shock. He asked if they were adopted, and Roberto said no, that they had all come naturally from Ana. The doctor did not believe Roberto.

Hours went by, and Ana eventually gave birth to a baby boy. They named him Giovanni. The doctors were in disbelief, as both Ana and Giovanni were healthy. The doctor's jaws dropped when Roberto brought the rest of the family up to the hospital. He again said it was impossible for Ana to have kids. He eventually called the children the "miracle babies." He followed by advising my parents not to have any more children. He continued by saying they had somehow gotten lucky with five, but they might not be so lucky with six. Ana and Roberto replied by saying that it was all in God's hands and that they would follow the will that was set out for them. Ana and Roberto ended up having two more children: another boy named Maximilian and a baby girl named Fatima. They realized that God's will was for them to end at seven children.

My parents, Ana and Roberto, were given a plan that was set by God, and they followed it. Parenting, to them, is set by the belief of the parents. Trust was central to everything they taught their family. They believed in everything they did and to this day, they still do. They took their time to raise us, they questioned us the right way, and they gave us the right morals and ethics so that we could rationalize the world on our own. They taught us to ready ourselves and to be authentic. You see my parents did three things well: they reflected on there lives, created a purpose and took responsibility for it. They understood that they probably wouldn't change the world, but they did see that they could affect their household in a positive way to make the world a better place.

I learned from my parents that a household needed an established belief system. A common goal, a mission, something we all can grow and aspire towards. In our family, it was our faith in Christ and our mission to get to heaven. I believe this helped me form myself into focused young professional looking to achieve my goals. This helps youth grow in their roots at home, and it helps them become authentic to themselves. This also gave me the ability to forge my incredible true story. I believe my parents gave me the opportunity to create my story and to allow it to be as unique as theirs.

# Chapter 3: Travel

*"Travel for the young is a part of education, For the old, a part of experience."*

—Francis Bacon

My dad believed that seeing the world was a great way to open us up to new possibilities. He always said, "You can't learn to appreciate what you have until you know how everyone else lives." He wanted to nourish his children's talents and bring out the best in us so that we could contribute to the world. My father saw us settling into the small-town Oklahoma life, but he wanted to break the routine, and he believed that traveling was a learning process to exploit something far more significant in a person's mind. His philosophy was that everything was art and that one could learn from everything in life. When he took trips by himself or with my mom in their early years, he witnessed a world far more significant than what he witnessed in Mexico, California, and Oklahoma. He thought more critically, solved problems better, understood other people's point of view, and became culturally diverse. One of the biggest things he learned was perspective. He believed that the best way the people of the world could learn to understand each other was by looking at different points of view.

My dad saw us growing bored in our lives: He saw my older brothers getting into trouble and all the younger ones following right along in their footsteps. Boredom can be terrible because if you're bored, then your life becomes pointless and you begin to develop a purposeless life. My dad saw that beginning, and he decided to do something about it. He wanted us to find a higher meaning in our lives, he wanted us to find a purpose.

Phil Jackson, arguably the greatest coach to ever work in the NBA, made a point about boredom and breaking the cycle in his book *Eleven Rings: The Soul of Success*. During the Bulls' run for their third consecutive title, Phil explained that his biggest enemy during that season was boredom. They had just won back-to-back titles, and the daily life of the NBA can be, as he wrote, a "stultifying, mind-numbing experience." He states: "My goal was to get the players to break free from their confining basketball cocoon and explore the deeper, more spiritual aspects of life. By 'spiritual' I don't mean 'religious,' I mean the act of self-discovery that happens when you step beyond your conventional way of seeing the world." So, what does this mean? As Phil explains, "To make work meaningful, you need to align it with your true nature." Wayne Tisdale writes in *A Monk in the World*: "For work to be sacred, it must be concerned to our spiritual realization. Our work must represent our passion, our desire to contribute to the culture, especially to the development of others. By passion, I mean the talents we must share with others, the talents that shape our destiny and allow us to be of real service to others in the community."

My father believed that traveling was the way to wake us up to be better. He wanted us to open our minds to a bigger world. He wanted us to abandon the way we were living in order to live a life of purpose. However, for as long as I've been with him, my father has had an exciting way of doing things.

My father had a particular way of traveling. He was picky about what we took along with us. We could only take a limited number of belongings because throughout our time overseas we lived on the go. Every day was filled with the unexpected. We would get to one place, find a hotel or a hostel, book our stay for however long we decided to stay, and then explore that place on the go. To my dad, this was called "being prepared in an unprepared situation." He explained to us after our trips why he did this, saying that life itself is unexpected and that one day, it might all go according to plan, and the next day, it might be completely unplanned. He went further to explain that he deliberately put us in scenarios that would prepare us for the unexpected so we could learn to problem-solve on the spot and work well under pressure.

Another way he helped to develop us was through the art and history of different countries we explored. He wanted us to know the various rises and falls of the people who went through these lands to find inspiration. He wanted us to look at the architecture of the buildings so that we could open our minds to different sceneries of the world. Another way he taught us a lesson was when all the hotels or hostels were booked, or if we were traveling overnight. At times we spent the night in the car, an airport, or a train station. At these moments we learned to appreciate what we previously took for granted, and we found out so much about ourselves along the way.

We took many different trips, but for now, I'll only refer to the three major ones. I have been to Europe and Africa on three separate occasions, and in the process learned so much. Though these trips were facilitated by my parents, they helped us find ourselves, our values, our talents, our purpose and most importantly, God. My parents wanted us to understand the journey of life, and they wanted us to enjoy it. They wanted us to learn how to see things on a different level, in a more in-depth meaning, like the journey of life.

Holden Hill, the author of *Bring the Fire*, said, "If you don't maintain curiosity and imagination even in the small and ordinary things, the vibrancy of the big things will die. You have to fall in love with the journey of life and the beauty of all that surrounds you, or you'll get to the end of life only to realize fulfillment never existed in the glory, possessions, and awards you've accumulated—it existed along the journey of life, in every adventure you failed to enjoy."

My parents knew this, and they wanted to show us all the beauty of life. The greatest thing has been for me to fall in love with life and the journey because once you fall in love with it, your purpose in life becomes apparent and you decide to take responsibility for it, then your incredible true story will be set.

# Chapter 4: Identity

*"Do not wish to be anything but what you are,
And try to be that perfectly."*

*—Saint Francis de Sales*

Through my years, I have always said people should never look to change, because as people you don't change, you grow.

Identity is an important topic, especially in a young person's life. No, I am not talking about biological or physiological human identity; I don't believe I am an expert at that. No, I am talking about who you decide to be in life, I believe that is the more important question. A question that my parents hammered into me was what was it I wanted to be in life? What was it I wanted to be known for? What was I going to do? These questions take time to reflect on.

Growing up, my answer to that question changed. The idea of what I wanted to be – who I wanted to be – developed and matured. At first, I said a wrestler because I use to watch WWE, then I got into boxing, so then I said boxing. I was a fighter. Eventually I grew out of that phase, then, after a while, I said I wanted to be Iron Man. I wanted to be smart like him, and build the first Iron Man suit. All valid ideas, but none of them were me. Growing up, it's OK to change what you want to be, and it's OK to question yourself. Questions always lead to answers.

It's very important to discover yourself. This part of a person's incredible true story is important. Who you want to be is very, very important. What's truly incredible my friends is that you can be whoever you decide to be. This is what I learned from my journey. Identity is dependent on the single most beautiful action God gave us: choice. What made discovering my identity so remarkable is how I grew and learned over time. Accepting who you are is just fine, but growth in who you are is something that I learned is incredibly important. This part of my story is essential to my incredible true story. To choose the path and to own it. This is essential for us all, because once we stand tall and proud for who we are, we inspire others to do so as well.

I first encountered my identity in Jerusalem when I learned what my name means. That's where I chose who I wanted to be.

# Jerusalem

We flew into Tel Aviv, Israel and my father rented a car, and drove us to Jerusalem to spend the night. I was walking through the Old City late at night, as we were searching for a place to stay. My father had a place where he wanted to stay, a hostel in the Old City, where he had stayed once before. However, we arrived there late—midnight, to be exact. We found the hostel, but when we walked in the lobby, I didn't see anyone at the front desk, but over the counter, there was a little man from India. The way everything was presenting itself to us, it seemed like we were in a fictional world. There was a receptionist the size of a dwarf, the hostel was built like a cave, and this was all located in the Old City of Jerusalem. We spoke to the man, and he was a fascinating character. He made fun of the way we presented ourselves. At one point, my backpack hit his lap, and it almost fell over, but I was able to catch it in time, and he replied to me, "Don't take my lap, I like this one." I laughed a bit because this man was very intriguing. He spoke to us about his time in Israel and how much he loved the women there and how great the food was and a number of other things.

During the process to get our room, he needed an ID. We gave him our passports, and as he looked through them, he commented on each of our names. He yelled out loudly, "Ramsel, Xcaret, Roberto!" and then he made remarks to my siblings and my father about their names, mispronouncing them, of course. When he got to my name "Baruc!" he kept saying my name, in different tones. I moved forward to see what he had to say about my name, and he leaned close and asked me if I knew what my name means. I replied, no. He then told me that in his land, my name means "good news," and in the greater Middle East, my name means "blessed."

He smiled and asked if I was "good news," and I replied with a big yes. Now, I was feeling good—my name meant something great! I was on a high at that moment. But self-doubt crept in and then I started to reflect: "Am I really good news?" So many questions came into my head at that time. Was I a good son? A good friend? Was I kind to others? Later, I asked my dad if he and my mom knew what my name meant when they gave it to me. He said yes, and that they believed I could live up to it. In that moment, I felt like they had determined an identity for me already. In a sense, I had to live up to the name. However, my dad told me that I could be whoever I want to be because my identity is based on my choice and how I would develop my choice overtime.

After I thought about it for a while, my parents named me Baruc for the simple reason that I would decide to be that of what my name means. I chose that day to be good news. I wanted people to think of me when good news came. When people heard my name, I wanted them to feel like it was good news. I didn't know how I was going to do that, all I knew was that my identity was who I decided to be in life. Moreover, who I decided to be was simply Baruc.

# Chapter 5: Perspective

*"I like to turn things upside down, to watch pictures and situations from another perspective."*

*—Ursus Wehrli*

I believe a person telling their incredible true story is essential, on the simple fact that it gives people perspective. Giving people perspective is the primary key to relate and build relationships in a community. Perspective is critical in life. Perspective is to paint a picture and have others understand your masterpiece. However, perspective can also be a new world that others never knew existed, and that's what makes a person's incredible true story so glorious.

Perspective is the beautiful look on life that all humans have. It allows us to understand others. However, it also gives us the ability to channel that perspective in order to help us overcome our obstacles, to honestly say "I can do this, other humans have and I can too." What I mean by this is, growing up I would go through certain challenges, if it was scoring high on my test, doing great at work, or challenging myself personally to do more in life. At times when I would think I couldn't do it, I always thought about my dad and his childhood. I'd always tell myself that he's overcome worse and if he can, then I can. Perspective allows us to reflect on others life's and challenges.

Perspective is such an incredible gift to humanity, but unfortunately, we don't use it. It was a vital part of my story because it enabled me to realize I could use it as a tool to understand others. I figured perspective allowed me to see worlds I had never experienced before. I believe talking about perspective and giving you an inside to my perspective in my journey would possibly open you to a new adventure.

I found perspective to be especially crucial in Egypt; I encountered a man and an obstacle that gave perspective in my life a new meaning.

# The Man in the Tent

We arrived at Mount Sinai. It was 11:30 p.m. in Egypt, and we were beaten up and exhausted from the journey there. From the border of Egypt to Mount Sinai, the trip took about six hours. We had arrived in what was known as the Fox Camp, a hotel right under Mount Sinai. For those of you who don't know, Mount Sinai is the mountain that Moses climbed, and where he saw God's back, as recorded in the book of Exodus in the Bible. The crazy part was that we never planned on stopping there. Our original plan was to travel from the Egyptian border and drive straight to Cairo, but the trip was way too long and so we decided to stop at Mount Sinai and rest for the night.

As we arrived at the camp, they took us into a tent. They had built a tent around a fire, where they would brew their tea and gather. In the tent, we found a man—a fascinating man from Belgium; He was a character! Every time he spoke, I found him to be strange. He spoke about many things; his religion, what he was doing in Egypt, his views on life. He shared to us why he had come to Mount Sinai. He told us the earth and sun had spoken to him and told him to make a pilgrimage from the tip of Israel to Egypt, and so he grabbed his things and began his walk from the tip of Israel to Egypt. He journeyed through the desert and made his way to Mount Sinai. My dad and this man spoke about religion and their views of life, but what I found so amusing was how they were so open to learning from each other. My dad was looking through the man's perspective, and the man was looking through my dad's perspective. By the end of the night, my dad had made a new friend. The man loved the stories my dad told him about my family and my dad's life. In turn, my dad found the man's stories exciting and knowledgeable. When we went to our rooms, my dad told us, "The only way we as people grow is to question life and see things from different perspectives. You can unravel your mind and understand life better if you engage in conversations like the one I was just in." It got me thinking that if I consider others' perspectives to be valuable like my dad did with that man's perspective then I probably would have been in a much more mature stage in my life.

# Climbing the Mountain

The lights turned on, and my eyes flew open. I didn't know what was happening, but my body got up. Moving like a zombie, I got dressed, thinking it was time to go. I was told to dress in warm clothes because I was going to climb the mountain. It was 3 a.m. and if we wanted to make it before sunrise, we had to leave as soon as possible. Making our way up the mountainside, my dad spoke to us about the climb. He told us to think about our lives and to let this be an example of persevering through challenges and making it to the top. During the climb, all I could think about was my comfortable bed, the comforts of my home, and my mom's warm embrace. It was finally coming into my head that this was both unnatural and uncomfortable. I was missing my home. I thought about my friends and family, I thought about my life, and I thought about my future. It was coming to me all at once. It was strange to me because I had never thought about any of this during my time in Oklahoma. I was beating myself up, feeling sorry for myself. My life sickened me. I was on the trip of a lifetime, but I was complaining about all of it in my head. I thought to myself, *how ungrateful can I be?*

I started thinking about how much of a jerk I was to my parents and my siblings. I thought about how selfish I was and how I took so many things for granted. I saw myself falling into a dark hole of hatred, and I knew I would never make it out. I was terrified of what I was becoming. I was fighting a battle in my mind, and all I could feel was my sister, Xcaret wrapping her arm around my head and asking me, "If I get tired, you'll carry me, right?" I smiled and said, "Yeah!" confidently, and at that moment, I realized I wasn't alone on this journey. I started thinking again about all of my family, friends, teachers, and supporters. I knew that they were counting on me to get back home and be a different person, especially my mom. I could not let her down. Through this struggle, I decided I would climb the mountain and that the mountain would become the symbol of my life. I would get to the top and be a different person when I saw the sun come up.

Midway through the climb, my legs were getting tired, but I kept forcing myself to keep going. I was desperate for a break, so we stopped. On the way up the mountain, the Egyptians had set up tents all along the paths. We found a resting point, and my brother reminded me that Moses had completed this climb, too.

My brother Ramsel told me the story of Moses. The prophet had been searching for his sheep that had strayed away from the herd. In the process, Moses saw a burning bush—but the bush was not burned up. He went to see why, and from within the burning bush, God spoke to him. God commissioned Moses to go free His people from the Pharaoh of Egypt. Later, Moses said to God, "If it is You, then let me see You." However, God told Moses that if he laid eyes on the Lord, then he would die, and so God allowed the prophet to see His back. At that moment, Moses saw all the vast landscapes and beauties of nature and was overwhelmed.

My dad turned to us and told us that we might be in for a surprise when we got up the mountain. He told us to put ourselves in Moses' place and understand that God was calling us to do something big in our lives. Right then and there I considered how coincidental this trip was. Going to Mount Sinai was not planned in the trip, climbing that mountain wasn't planned at all. In Moses' story, I'm pretty sure he never thought he would lose a sheep. God wanted him to climb that mountain for a reason. God wanted me to climb that mountain as well and to ultimately put myself in Moses' shoes. In that moment, I realized neither of our journeys were coincidental. All I could do was pray and prepare myself for whatever was coming my way in the future.

As we made our way to the top, we were racing the sun to see who could make it to the top of the mountain first. I was determined to find the answers to my life on the top of the mountain. We were almost there—until Xcaret and Dad got tired. They didn't want to keep going, I begged them to continue, but they couldn't. It was too cold, and they were tired. I had made it so far that I didn't care how cold or tired I was. Nothing was going to stop me from making it to the top. Ramsel and I made our way to the top. I was full of emotion. I had never witnessed a sight so marvelous in my life. Instead of seeing what everyone perceived as mountains and the sun, right then and there I "became" Moses and I witnessed, with my own eyes, God's back. The sun was coming out, and a few tears fell from my eyes; my perspective had changed. I saw things differently, and I was happy. The realization of this journey was me recognizing and overcoming the obstacles of my life. I had overcome so many obstacles on my way to the top, and I now realized that my life was the mountain—and I had made it to the top. From start to finish, I completely changed from being homesick to making it my mission to persevere and get to the top.

God spoke to me through that journey. He showed me that I was made for greatness—not for comfort.

At the end of the trip, my dad asked me what I learned. I told him that perspective could be anywhere—not just in people, but in places, as well. A person can climb the mountain and see a cool sunrise, but if they don't change their perspective, it will be like any other sunrise. I changed my perspective and put myself in place of Moses—and I encountered God. I learned that perspective incites reflection which then unravels your mind with knowledge and understanding but also with purpose.

# Chapter 6: Grateful for Your Generosity

*"The wicked are always ungrateful."*

*—Miguel de Cervantes*

Throughout my incredible true story, I've learned several lessons. My first lesson centered around the question: "How grateful and generous am I about the things in my life?" My incredible true story opened my eyes to something that I had always ignored: gratefulness and generosity.

My time in Egypt woke me up. I've visited the country twice, and both times, I was humbled by what I saw. The trips shook me awake to what I was missing—that a person must never be ungrateful. If one is ungrateful, then it destroys the significance of life, because once you start being grateful for what you have instead of taking it for granted, life gets so much better. To be ungrateful is not to be generous, and that leads to an purposeless life.

Walking through the land of the Egyptians, I saw children with hardly any clothes. I saw mothers pulling food out of the trash to eat. I saw fathers seemingly embarrassed and humiliated as their family watched them beg for money just to survive. How much of a struggle were these people enduring? I had been blinded in Oklahoma that the world had far greater problems than trying to get a new Xbox. There was a time when we were walking through a square in Cairo, and a child saw my brother's pen and begged for it. He said he needed it for school. I stood there and reflected: "How much of what I have am I truly grateful for?" I thought about all the times I had yelled at my parents for not buying me what I wanted. I remembered all the times when I had gotten something, but it wasn't enough. I thought about all the times when I had become jealous of what my friends had. At the same time, I stood there thinking to myself how grateful am I for what I had at that very moment – how grateful I was for having the clothes I was wearing, for having the opportunities I had been given, and for the people I knew and loved. I felt so disgusted with myself, and I hated what I had become. Life was ugly to me. I never knew how rich I was until I saw with my own eyes the lives of others that had virtually nothing. It was then, through understanding the people of Egypt, that I truly recognized how ungrateful I had been.

During my time in Egypt, my parents began to ask me questions, and they began to make me think. The first questions they threw at me were "How grateful are you?" and "How generous are you?" and "How have you affected others?" and "What will you do differently when you go home?" and "How will you act toward life now?" All of these are valid questions to ask, and I was at the point that I had to make a change. Would I succumb to what I was becoming—a greedy, ungrateful, snotty child? Or, was I going to take the challenge that God brought upon me and change who I was becoming?

When you destroy yourself by not being grateful, your actions become motivated by hate instead of generosity. Being grateful correlates with being generous; you can't be one without the other. Once you find yourself doing both, then life becomes more significant, beautiful, and much more joyful which the byproduct is purpose. I believe that God proposes generosity as the path for happiness. The world proposes selfishness as the path to happiness— and that is wrong. God teaches us to be kind and understand what we have. He encourages us to spread our fruit to the world.

This is the world in which we live, and we're all brothers and sisters. We must learn to take care of each other and begin to appreciate what we have, because to find purpose we must be generous, and generosity begins with gratitude.

During my time in Egypt, I witnessed greed and selfishness, but I also witnessed humility and generosity. Many poor people, of course, wanted more than what they had, and they would steal or kill to get what they needed. I also saw people who were grateful for what little they had. I saw people share and take care of each other. They knew that the only way to survive was if they lived for one another. I witnessed beauty in these actions. The Egyptian people humbled me. They brought me to realize that I had plenty and that I should always work for others.

After our trips to Egypt, my dad and mom started asking me, "What are you doing?" At first, I didn't understand, but they came back with, "What are you doing to help these people?" I noticed that when I put my own selfish needs over everything, I lost sight of the world's most significant problems. For instance, the greatest problem in Egypt and all over the world is poverty. There is plenty of food around the world to feed us all, yet there are men, women, and children who are in a constant state of starvation. So, I come back to the question: "What are you doing?" As people who have enough, we must take care of those who don't. Once we're grateful, then we must begin to be generous to others.

The ultimate transformation happens when you stop trying to get, and instead start focusing on giving. You are at your best when you are giving! I was focused on what I wasn't getting; I was not focused on what I was not giving. As humans, we cannot help everyone, but that is not an excuse for not trying. I always questioned my mom about why she continued to teach catechism at our parish, and she said, "If I can save one child, then I am fine with that. If I can get one child to heaven, then I am happy to do God's work." My mom's message was clear: Don't let your limitations interfere with what you can do. As humans, we must know what we have and be grateful so we can be generous and give back to those who have nothing. As my mom said to me, "Those who have much, God asks of them to give more back." To be generous is not just something we're supposed to do, but it is a purpose rooted in who we are, once you are aware of this a purposeful life starts to form. But generosity must be the center of our human values, and we must think in terms of how we can do good at all times. To find true purpose within ourselves and humanity, let's be grateful and share our generosity to the world.

So, if you genuinely want to live your best life today, tomorrow, and for the rest of your life, you must come to the conclusion that you have to live to serve others. That's how you change lives, that's how you change the world, and that's how you become the best you that you can be. That is the message for my first lesson. My incredible true story led me to this truth.

# Chapter 7: Family

*"A happy family is but an earlier heaven."*

*—George Bernard Shaw*

In my incredible true story, my family has played a significant role. My family is my roots. I would do everything for my family. In my incredible true story, I wanted to recognize the people in my life that have helped me become the person I am today. Family doesn't necessarily mean your parents and brothers and sisters –your family can range from aunts, uncles, cousins, and grandparents to friends, neighbors, and community. Whoever has been there for you in your best or worst –that's your family. My incredible true story has led me to believe family holds an essential position in human purpose.

Family is at the center of all life. The nourishment of a family dictates how those people will love, care, serve, and lead the world. I say this because, in my opinion, the value of family cannot be overstated. It's the first opportunity for a child to learn social life, it's the first opportunity for a child to learn how to love, it's the first opportunity for the child to learn how to treat others, and so on. From the moment of birth, children need acceptance, love, esteem, spiritual and emotional support, and the material comfort that makes a healthy childhood possible. Through this, we can grow future leaders that can nourish the world as their families nourished them. With the nourishment of family, we take the first step toward world peace.

Make no mistake, no family is perfect. Families will endure hardships and struggles, but only when families come together can they continue to grow. Through the family, a child can learn how to overcome problems. The family is the first community to which a person belongs. If the community at home is broken, then that can only lead to a broken society. However, if a child sees the struggle in a family, but the outcome is unity and partnership, then the child grows to learn how to solve problems, and the home community grows stronger through love and unity. A family is a responsibility that we must be critical of personally and collectively. To have a family is to practice to two human liberties: freedom and love. To which freedom and love are nothing without responsibility.

The mission of a family is to create an atmosphere where love can flourish. Family creates a world of great possibilities. A family is a support system, where children and parents can evolve into more exceptional beings. It is vital for families to grow and show values of charity, purity, love, selflessness, and devotion. From this, we can go out into the world and build families outside of our homes. With that, we come closer to solving our world problems: racism, homicide, incarceration, and any other problem that stands in the way society's progress. It all begins at home.

The communion of a family is unbreakable. That is why it's permanent. The love of a family is essential for one to grow. If the love is there, then the child can fully develop into a person who can love others well. The love of a family is the key to love in society. The family is the cornerstone of human society. When the love of the first human society is healthy, then it is carried into the society of the world.

Family equality can serve as a path to equality in society. The way a household is run is essential, and how parents share responsibility and decision-making is very important. I believe that it teaches children how to treat others: equally and with respect. One is affected by the way a man treats a woman, a child's actions are dictated by the way their parents treated each other, and through that, they will carry it on to their families and other people. Families also must be open to learning from their children, as well. A woman at my church once told me, "We adults learn from our children as much as they learn from us." Also, Christ once said, "Amen, I say to you, unless you turn and become like children, you will not enter the kingdom of heaven" (see Matthew 18). A child and a woman have as much to offer to a family as the patriarch of the family. Through equality of the household, we develop a better sense of equality that we can then apply in relationships with our fellow peoples of the world. Through this, we break the ugly sin of discrimination. Families need to cultivate an environment where they can absorb positive feedback to contribute to their daily lives outside of the home. Through a safe home atmosphere, a family becomes a cocoon for a child to evolve and blossom in the world. As I mentioned before, a family must be something we need to be critical of and be responsible for. We find that the first and most crucial step into ushering in world peace is dependent on the very core of life: the family.

My family has always been the foundation of the choices that I make, and I believe this story will tell you why.

# Together

In the movie *Avengers: Age of Ultron*, there is a scene in which Ultron, the antagonist of the movie, is created and tells the Avengers his goal for world extinction and attacks the Avengers. After Ultron escapes from the Avengers and leaves to grow stronger and expand his plot, the Avengers meet to talk about Ultron and why he was created. Ultron was created by Tony Stark (Iron Man) and Bruce Banner (Hulk), and in the process of creation, Ultron takes over their systems and creates himself. Tony Stark had the vision to have a suit of armor with A.I. to fly around the world to eliminate potential threats. All the other Avengers argued against him, but he insisted that it could be a way to better protect the world from anything that could come from outer space. He ended his argument by asking Captain America how he planned on fighting any threat that would come toward earth, if not with Ultron. Captain America said, "Together," and Tony responded with, "We'll lose," and Captain America said, "We'll do that together, too." Later on during the movie, Ultron has grown, and the Avengers are surrounded by an army of Ultrons. Ultron asked them how he planned on defeating him, and Tony replied, "Just like the old man said, together." In that instance, the scene really spoke to me because that "all for one, one for all" attitude is how I look at my family. We succeed and fail together, we fight and love together, we are born and die together, and we grow and live together.

On our second and last trip as a family together, we were halfway through the trip, and we were growing homesick and tired of traveling. We were all in a bad mood, and we would often turn on each other. We were headed to Medjugorje, Bosnia. This is a holy place, as it is said that our lady, the Virgin Mary, appeared to children there and unveiled to them ten secrets of the future. Medjugorje was a place of conversion and peace. Before getting there, though, our family got into a major fight. We weren't talking to each other, and we were all defeated by sin.

Arriving at Medjugorje, my dad parked outside the church and went to listen to mass by himself. While we waited in the car, we started opening up a bit with each other. We felt like we needed to be with Christ if we were going to enjoy our time in Medjugorje and get the full experience. We all went our separate ways and began to pray. Eventually, we all got in line to confess our sins. We started feeling better and secure with each other again. Medjugorje became a place where we all were bathed in the mercy and glory of Christ and His mother. Throughout our days there, we all went our separate ways in prayer. We began to find ourselves and our reason for this trip. We began to find the advantages of traveling again. We were able to talk with each other again and start pulling back together as a family.

When New Year's Eve came around, my sister and I went to walk around the little town. She said that she wanted to buy treats and gather our family in our room to be together for the New Year. So, she bought treats and told everybody to meet in her room at ten-thirty at night to be together. When ten-thirty came around, we were all together as a family. We all sat up together and started telling stories about our lives and past trips we had taken. We were enjoying each other's presence and laughing at the stories that were being told. Spending time together had gotten us to appreciate one another. Then, my mom started telling us the story of how she and my dad had met – when they got married, and all about their lives. They spoke of their testimonies of love and passion for one another. Also, they spoke about the time when each of us was born. They ended with telling us about their passion for life; everything they did was for us. We were their greatest creation and that nothing would ever get in the way of our family

When times get rough, the family should be the priority. It doesn't matter what happened to us; nothing would ever tear us apart because we share the bond of blood under Christ. Our parents told us to look around the room and look at each other—because we were all that we had and we had to stay together for all of time. When the clock struck twelve, we ended our night by saying the rosary; then we all hugged each other and went to bed.

. At that time, I reflected on the sacrifices and responsibilities that my parents took when they decided to create a family, my conclusion is this:

 no family is perfect, but that is no excuse to fall apart. We all go through life, but at the end of the day what we have is family. Your family, the people who are there, if it's a parent, sibling, friend or community, those are the first people we meet when we are brought into this world, and they are the people with whom we grow up until we leave our homes to make a family of our own. Your family members are the first ones to greet you when you are born, and your family members are the last to bid you farewell when your time has come. Having a family on earth is to genuinely experience a form of heaven on earth.

# Chapter 8: Blessings

*Our prayers should be for blessings in general, for God knows best what is good for us.*

*—Socrates*

In my incredible true story, some stories are unique to me. What I mean by this is that no one can really relate to or comprehend simply because they are life miracles, or how I like to call them, blessings. These are the stories that make my incredible true story different from the rest, to show the world that the impossible is possible. These stories can't be explained but only told, because these stories are the stories that allow us to see that the world is filled with so much more than what is comprehendible, but instead will always be a mystery, and it's these stories that make life worth living.

I witnessed so many blessings; there was no way I could define who or what was causing them. I believe it was God, but to others, it is pure will and strength. I believe a blessing is a contribution of hard work and God's grace. These stories show what I genuinely believe are a combination of both.

# Christmas in Bethlehem

My dad wanted to do something different. He thought it would be cool to be in the Holy Land—in Bethlehem—at Christmas time. We were already in the Holy Land during the Christmas season, which is probably the busiest time for tourism Israel experiences besides Easter, however, my dad had it all figured out. He planned to arrive on Christmas week and take it by the day. That was probably the worst plan ever because everyone goes to Israel during Christmas and everything is usually booked. Fortunately for us, my dad was able to find a tiny hostel in the Old City where we stayed for three days. We were running out of time, Christmas was approaching, and we realized that we might have to sleep in the car for Christmas Eve and Christmas Day.

We spent the day in crowded Bethlehem, there were people everywhere. You couldn't take a step without being shoulder-to-shoulder with someone else. All the streets were filled with people preparing for the celebration of the birth of Christ. Bethlehem is small, and they throw a festival on the night of Christmas in the town square, which everyone attends. They close down the Church of the Nativity and let all of the people celebrate. My dad's plan was to be in the Church of the Nativity when the clock struck midnight, so we could pray and be together at the time when the Lord our Savior was brought into the world. Now, that would have been a great experience, but that did not happen.

Night came, and the hectic sounds of the party were coming from the town square. We were standing there, looking lost. We didn't have any idea what to do. What we had come for what was closed, and we didn't feel safe going to the party in the town square. My dad chose to start looking for a place to stay the night. He started browsing the Internet and called all of the inns near us, but he kept getting rejections telling him that they were all booked for the next few days. We were starting to lose hope that we would find a place to stay. Then my dad called his friend from Poland to ask if he could help look for a place. My dad never gave up; he kept calling place after place, asking them for any help. His only mission was to get his family into beds and to keep them safe. Now, the rest of us were doing nothing in the car. We were sitting there waiting to hear the news that we were going to have to sleep in the car. Then my mom gathered us together to pray. We all came together and gave thanks to the Lord. We thanked Him for allowing us to be in Bethlehem on the night that He was born, and we ended the prayer by accepting the consequence of not being prepared and booking a room in advance. I remember our final prayer went: "Lord, if it is Your will for us to sleep in the car, then so be it. We will still give You thanks for protecting us and allowing us to have a place to stay." It took about five minutes to receive a blessing from the Lord. We received a call from a Catholic nun convention that hosted families all year long. They called to tell us that three rooms had just opened up because the couples who had booked them had called to say that they wouldn't be there until the next night. My dad immediately took the rooms with no hesitation, and right after that, we were off. I remember we went through the crowds, asking people to point us in the right direction. It was so strange that everything was falling into place. Everyone we asked was helpful, but it all made sense. This was our blessing from God.

We arrived at the convention, and the nuns greeted us with a whole dinner prepared for us. My dad told them that he didn't have the money to pay anything extra for the meals and they replied by saying, "God has blessed you tonight with all you need, do not worry." Those words have stuck with me forever. An hour before, we had been preparing to sleep in the car, and now, out of nowhere, we had found a place to eat dinner and sleep. We were truly blessed that night. My father cried at the table during grace; he didn't believe we deserved that blessing. We sat together eating, enjoying each other's presence and delighting in the day of the Lord. I believe that this was a blessing from God. I believe that blessings are a combined effort of action, prayer and need. Through this experience, I concluded that we were experiencing what Mary and Joseph had experienced on the night of Christmas when Christ was born. They searched for a place to stay that night in Bethlehem, and they received rejection after rejection, but they prayed and believed in the mission of God, and, in the end, received the greatest blessing of all…Christ.

# Santorini

We were leaving Turkey angry with each other. My sister had declared to my family that she didn't want to go to Europe this time around. It put us all in a bad mood, and we started off the trip fighting. It was very ungrateful of us as well because we were overseas as a family traveling the world and we were angry at the fact that we didn't want to be there.

Greece was our next destination, and we were headed to Santorini, a small island in the Aegean Sea. We had booked a hotel for a few days there, and my dad hoped it would serve as a retreat for us until we went back to traveling from country to country. We arrived, comfortably settled into our rooms, and got ready to explore the town. My sister decided to stay in her room and not go out with us, and that brought us down even more. We could feel a family disaster fast approaching and we still had almost a whole month to go in Europe.

The days went by, and we reached our final day on the island. It was a Sunday, and my dad wanted us to find a Catholic church to attend service before we left. It wasn't hard to locate one because the island was so small. Within a few minutes, we arrived at the church. We walked in to find an entire community eating in a room at the parish. We ran into many Latinos at that parish; it seemed very strange. The parish priest, a Mexican named Father Paco, proceeded to greet us. We all looked at each other—it seemed very strange—but they welcomed us. They gave us food and hospitality, asking us where we were from and why we were visiting Santorini, and so on. Father Paco asked why we had wandered in, and we told him we wanted to listen to mass before we left. He told us he had just finished the last mass. We were saddened—but he had a better idea. He offered to hold a private mass and a blessing for us. He gathered us into the church and began to bless us. He gave us a small talk and spoke beautifully to us as if he had known us his whole life. He went on to talk about the importance of the family and why it was so important to stay together. Then he reached the end of the service, and he spoke to us about the trouble he sensed in our hearts. We were all in tears at that moment; we saw the incredible opportunity that we had been given. We had each other and the love of God. This service transformed us and the rest of the trip, and we found ourselves in each other. Through the blessing of Christ, we were able to come together as a family again.

We thought the blessings were over after that, but following our private mass, Father Paco invited us to eat. He took us to the most expensive restaurant in Santorini and covered the bill for everything. We met his mother, his sister, and his brother at dinner. They told us about their lives and why they had come to Greece. We were so captivated by their story, and we were so grateful for what they had done for us. They brought us in and gave us a home. When our time on the island came to an end, Father Paco took us to the airport and saw us off. We left Santorini with our hearts filled with the love of one another and God.

Christ sends blessings in all forms and types of situations, and even though we might be experiencing hardships with our families, in making a tough decision, or even in times of joy, Christ lives in all things in our lives. As humans, we must never forget to look for Him in these times because we can fall if we don't. We could have fallen and thrown away such an expensive trip, but we found Christ and He appeared to us as a blessing in Father Paco.

Look for the good in everything, because I can promise you that a blessing lives in every aspect of life.

# Chapter 9: Hospitality

*True hospitality consists of giving the best of yourself to your guest.*

*—Eleanor Roosevelt*

Hospitality was one of the incredible lessons I learned on my journey, during my Incredible True Story one of the purposes I found rooted in the human is service. One way you can have a significant impact on people is through the simple act of inviting someone over to your home and being hospitable – serving them and allowing them to feel at home. However, this isn't just applied in homes, but also in classrooms, schools, colleges, jobs, and the list can go on and on. However, hospitality isn't just making the atmosphere feel like home, but helping a person emotionally feel at home. When a person is with you, regardless of where you are at, allow them to feel safe, comfortable, and authentic. You can make a much more powerful impact by just being hospitable to another person and doing so through service. My friends, that is the true meaning of home.

Home is where the heart is, and I believe that humanity has a purpose and responsibility to represent the home in every aspect of life. To represent home to those who do not have a home, to represent home to those who struggle at home, and to represent home to those who are broken – we can only do this by serving the world.

So, invite people into your life, show them what you do, be a friend to them, and become a family for them. We must practice this virtue to begin the march for acceptance and love. We can only live freely if we open our lives, serve and bring love and respect to others.

During my various trips, I've witnessed hospitality on so many different levels, in so many different places. Keep this in mind, I was on the other side of the world, thousands of miles away from home, but because of the service I was given and the people I met, I felt right at home.

# Poland

As a Catholic, to me, Poland is holy ground. Poland saw a great demise during World War II and the subsequent Cold War, but since then, Poland has found its way to become a place full of hope and love. Our time in Poland was something incredible. Out of all the places I have traveled to, Poland has always been a home away from home. When we were in Poland, we were greeted so kindly. My dad has a friend named Sylvester who lives in Poland. Sylvester has a family that includes his wife Elizabeth and a daughter named Hanna. They are a beautiful family that travels often – even more than my family does. Sylvester asked my dad to bring our family to Poland for a visit for Christmas because a few years back, they had come to Mexico to spend Christmas with us.

Out of our three different trips, the visit to Poland was especially incredible and warming. The first time around we arrived at the beginning of January; on that trip, we spent Christmas on a train and the beginning of the new year in the lobby of a hotel—two of the worst experiences of my life. Arriving in Poland, it felt like we had just arrived at home. We were welcomed with open arms and a big dinner.      A few days in, Sylvester held a Christmas party with his friends, telling us that he wanted us to experience Christmas in Poland. He prepared a traditional dinner, and we all enjoyed the people who came to meet us, even so far away from home.

On that trip, we had another fantastic experience. We had just finished a long march in the cold, and we were all freezing—and wet. It was snowing and raining that day. After we finished our walk, Sylvester took us to a friend's house. When we arrived, they had clothes prepared for us to change into, washed our clothes and then cooked for us. The mom of the family treated us like her own, and I saw a lot of my mom in her. It was incredible because she could not even speak English, but she communicated with us through her hospitality. Leaving their home later, we sat in the car and talked about how we felt like we were back at home. We left Poland, having had an enjoyable experience.

# Poland 2.0

The last two times we visited Poland, we went as a family. Have you ever seen or read, *The Hobbit*? Well, in the story, there is a part where all thirteen dwarves arrive at Bilbo's home, but they arrive at different times, and they eat all of Bilbo's food and trash his house. That scene in *The Hobbit* reminds me of how we presented ourselves to other families that invited us into their homes. We visited several homes because they invited us, but in Europe, the family size is typically four people or less; five is too many. We weren't trashy or messy but we are a big family for sure.

When we visited, these families were serving a family size of nine. In these two trips combined, we visited seven different small homes. Those nights, they cooked so much food with so many different courses, and so many outstanding desserts. Sylvester mentioned to us that that was the most they had ever cooked in their lives. It was so funny because there were so many of us—and a big family is a loud family. It must have been so overwhelming for the them; they didn't know how to contain all of us, but what they did do was make us feel at home. They allowed us to express ourselves freely. It was fascinating how these families reacted to us; they weren't used to a family that was so big and loud, but they served us so well. They showed us so much love and care, and all we could do was to thank them. They opened their homes to us when they didn't have to. We were people who didn't even live in the same country, who didn't speak the same language, and who aren't even the same ethnicity, but they still treated us like their own. They brought our Oklahoma home to Poland for us, and they did that through hospitality. That is the incredible thing about hospitality—that you can bring your home anywhere if you treat others with equality and love.

# Brother

It was my first trip overseas, and I was scared and excited. I feared to leave home, but I was excited to see all the wonders of the world. I had these feelings throughout the whole trip—but it all changed in Israel. We were in the lobby of a hotel in Jerusalem, just having gotten back from Egypt. We were sitting there, hanging out, waiting for our room to be ready. My dad got on the computer, but he encouraged us to talk to the people around us. My brother and sister weren't interested; they were tired and just wanted to sleep. However, I was sitting there, still amazed at what I had just experienced in Egypt. A guy was sitting next to me, and I'm sure he overheard what my dad told us. This middle-aged man, who was probably in his late twenties or early thirties, started talking to me. He asked me my name and where I was from, and I replied. I told him my name and that I was from America—but that my ethnicity was Hispanic. When he introduced himself, he told me that he was from the Netherlands. A few words turned into a friendly chat.

We were asking each other why we were there and what we hoped to gain from our travels. Then he asked what I wanted to be when I grew up. At the time, I wanted to be an engineer like Iron Man, and that's what I told him. He laughed, but he recommended a few books for me to read about my future profession. After a few more minutes of talking, he had to go. However, he told me why he had started talking to me in the first place: I reminded him of his little brother. We shook hands, and he said, "Goodnight, my brother, I'll see you around."

I saw that man one more time. The following morning, he was leaving with his bags packed. He said to me, "I had a great time talking to you last night. I hope you enjoy your time here in Israel. Farewell, *mi hermano* (my brother in Spanish)." After that, I never saw him again, but that man remains in my memories. I will never forget the hospitality that he showed me. In those few brief moments, he became family to me, and I became family to him. We were from two different parts of the world, but we were able to make Israel our home together because we shared the bond of brotherhood.

The next time I went to Israel, when I looked at that hotel, I only saw my brother. Whatever it is that we do for strangers, good or bad, know that it will echo throughout their lives. This man's hospitality to this day echoes in my life.

# Medjugorje

Medjugorje has been a home away from home to my family. When I visited there for the first time, it was not the first time for my older siblings and my parents. In the small town of Medjugorje, there is a home where we stayed. Back in the day when people would conduct pilgrimages there, they would have to lodge at the homes of the residents. There were no hotels at that time. Today, there are many hotels because Medjugorje has since become a haven for tourists. However, every time my family visited Medjugorje, we stayed in a home with a family. When we stayed there, I experienced firsthand the hospitality of this family.

It is incredible to me that over time, this family still remembers my parents. One of the reasons my time at Medjugorje was such a blessing in my life was because of that family. We arrived at their home asking for rooms, and in addition to the rooms, they gave us big hugs and fed us breakfast, lunch, and dinner every single day. They made sure we were ready for each day by providing bottles of water and extra sweaters in case it was too cold for us. They were like our grandparents, always making sure we had whatever we needed for our day. They only showed us humility and love. I only saw good and no evil. I believed that they were angels sent from heaven to take care of us. Their hospitality was from heaven. This family changed our outlook on the idea of family, they changed our view on how to treat others, and they brought us closer to Christ with just their hospitality.

On our last day there, they prepared lunches and gave us drinks for our journey to Italy. My dad tried to pay them for their extra service to us, but they only wanted below the minimum payment from us. They told my dad, "Why in the world would we charge a family to stay at our home?" My dad could not believe what they had said. They so blessed us, our new extended family in Medjugorje.

It is incredible how humanity can change for the better through hospitality. Being able to bring a sense of hope to the lives of other people is so essential, and through this, we can live in brotherhood and peace with one another. When we bring a sense of home to each other's lives, we learn to respect, but we also learn how to love. Through this, we begin to change lives, we begin to evolve, and we become better people. We were given this beautiful world called Earth, and all we have done is create separation and battlegrounds out of it. We have been called by God to build homes, to create a world filled with love. In conclusion within the purpose of service rooted in all of us, we find that we are subjects of love. Capable of great things. But what makes us subjects of love is that rooted within us is gratitude and service. As subjects of love we are capable of two things: to serve and to be served. This presents us with a conclusion that we as humans take objection to be looked as an object of use, therefore, we can rationalize and feel that to find human fulfillment within our purpose is through the acts of service and love.

So, I challenge you to practice the virtue of service, to go out and build homes in this world, and through this, we can bring peace into the lives of so many people.

# Chapter 10: Belief

*"If you do not live what you believe, you will end up believing what you live."*

— `Archbishop Fulton J. Sheen

In every incredible true story, one thing that's needed is belief. My belief in life is something very important. For me, I knew my religious beliefs were true, I just had to understand that I needed to live it and not necessarily seek a feeling from it.

My belief is what fueled my why (which we will get to). What I believe gave me a reason for why I do things. It gave me strength. It's my belief that gives me passion for what I do. It compelled me to new heights. It is my sole power, the strength that comes within.

I grew up Catholic. My dad gave me the option of allowing me to choose what I believe in when I turned 18. Leading up to it, I always believed in God. I had belief in the Catholic faith. However, there was no soul power, no conviction in me. In this part of my story, I had the chance to live my faith and truly walk alongside God. Through this part of my story, my "why" gained belief, passion, and soul power. Within this experience I found that there is no greater glory then to die for what you believe in. To believe in something other than yourself is critical in your human existence. One of the great responsibilities in life is your freedom. Your freedom to choose. Your freedom to believe in a higher purpose then yourself and to accept it. This part of my story is what makes my incredible true story so energetic and authentic to me.

# The Church of the Nativity

My first encounter with my faith was on my first trip overseas. At that time, I was there to check out the sites, visiting Israel and just enjoying my time there. To my surprise, I witnessed the experience of love and birth.

We had arrived in Bethlehem late, looking for a place to stay. We found a hotel and decided to settle in and then go out and explore the city more. The streets were small, everything was so crammed together, but the atmosphere was filled with joy. People were out and about, exploring the adventures that this small place had to offer. The significance of this city is that it is the city of Jesus's birth. Walking through town square, we saw a large church along the side, but the front door was tiny. My dad later told us that this was a symbol of reverence to the Lord, when you entered through the door you'd come in crouching, it looked like you were bowing down. We were entering the holy ground, and the architects wanted us to bow every time we stepped into the church.

The following day, we entered that church. It was big on the inside. The church was separated into two parts: the orthodox side and the Catholic/Christian side. We went through both sides, exploring and studying the details of the church. The room was mystical, had art of angels through the side leading up to the alter. The columns that held the build together were magnificent, they looked like pillars holding up a coliseum. The colors through the room were gold and bright. I really felt as if I stepped into a time machine. Around the altar of the Catholic side, there is a room into which people could go. In that room, it is said that Jesus was born and was laid there to rest in a manger. We didn't think we'd be able to go in that room because it was filled with people, but we persistently forced our way in. When we entered, we saw that there was a wedding taking place in that room. We stood there to see the couple consecrate their vows, and we witnessed the birth of new life faithfully. My heart and soul were filled with love, and the fact that I was able to touch the rock on which Christ had been laid brought me a moment that I'd never forget. At that very moment, belief in my faith was born.

Belief is the strength of the soul. Witnessing a marriage on the same piece of ground where Christ was born—that gave birth to my faith. I saw that couple profoundly consecrate their vows with so much belief in front of Christ. You could tell their belief in Christ gave them strength in why they were marrying each other. So much soul power and so much conviction filled that room. In that very moment I realized belief came from choice, a choice on what one wishes to believe and in the same motion work at what they believe in and live for what they believe in. At that moment, I chose to believe in Christ.

# Mount Tabor

When we arrived on Mount Tabor, my older brother encouraged us to be focused on prayer and dive into our faith life, and so I decided to give it a try. Mount Tabor is also known as the Mountain of Transfiguration. For those who don't know the story, Mount Tabor was where Jesus took Peter, John, and James, and during their time up on the mountain, Jesus's garments and appearance changed into full white, and he was seen speaking to Elijah and Moses. Peter, James, and John were each in disbelief and terrified of what was happening right in front of them, but a voice out of the sky said, "This is My Son, whom I love; with Him, I am well pleased. Listen to Him!" (Matthew 17:5)

Once we reached the top of the mountain, we spotted a beautiful church with a view that I will never forget. The church overlooked the lands of Israel, and the sun was beautifully shining down upon the entire countryside. I felt the holiness of this land, and I felt the presence of the Lord. We walked in to take a seat in the Church, and my brother read to us from the gospel of the Transfiguration, and then we prayed the rosary. While sitting there, I prayed to the Lord. I told Him that I was there and that I was ready to listen to Him, and at that point, I was able to experience the Transfiguration. When I saw the beautiful landscape, the church overlooked while I was praying, my heart felt at peace.

# Galilee

Galilee was like a resort, so beautiful and relaxing. Galilee was my favorite place in Israel, and we stayed in Tiberias, a city of the Sea of Galilee. We stayed there for a few days, and that was our place to recharge and relax. We were able to take a good break from all the moving and traveling. In Galilee, there are a few Christian landmarks, including Peter's home and the church where Christ first appeared to Peter. My older brother was very excited to visit those churches; Peter was his saint, the man he admired most in the Catholic Church. My brother was almost fan-girling over this. He knew the significance of these places, while I, on the other hand, had finally drawn interest since Mount Tabor, but I was still fighting it. I still didn't know what to do with my new sense of faith.

We had arrived at Peter's house. It wasn't much of a big deal at his home, the appearance wasn't that great; very small, it seemed like leftover ruins, but the fact that Peter had lived there was significant. On the other hand, the church that had been built along the shore of the Sea of Galilee—that was a whole different story. This church was the site where Jesus appointed Peter as the first pope in Matthew 16:18: "You are Peter, and on this rock, I will build my Church." At that point, Christ not only called Peter, but He called all of His followers to action. When my mom read that verse to me, she made it very clear that my belief was nothing without action to back it up. On Mount Tabor, my faith life was awakened, but on Galilee, it was strengthened and given direction. Once I found my belief, I figured one thing out: that I must go out into the world and teach what I believe. After Christ, Peter became the earthly head of the Church, and he led the Church. At that moment, God asked me to lead with my belief, just as Peter did.

# The Mountain of the Beatitudes

After visiting Galilee, I was eager for more. Christ had awakened a fire in my soul, and it was raging. What better place to ignite my flame than the place where Christ gave the most excellent sermon of all time: The Mountain of the Beatitudes. The church that had been built on top of this mountain overlooked all of Galilee. The scenery where Christ gave this sermon was breathtaking, the church is located on top of the highest hill overlooking other hills. The view from the top oversaw a landscape of green meadows that leads to the shiny sea of Galilee.

We walked into the church, sat down, and began reading in the gospel of Matthew, Chapter 5: "Blessed are the poor in spirit, for theirs is the kingdom of heaven. Blessed are they who mourn, for they will be comforted. Blessed are the meek, for they will inherit the land. Blessed are they who hunger and thirst for righteousness, for they will be satisfied. Blessed are the merciful, for they will be shown mercy. Blessed are the clean of heart, for they will see God. Blessed are the peacemakers, for they will be called children of God. Blessed are they who are persecuted for the sake of righteousness, for theirs is the kingdom of heaven. Blessed are you when they insult you and persecute you and utter every kind of evil against you [falsely] because of me. Rejoice and be glad for your reward will be great in heaven. Thus, they persecuted the prophets who were before you." In Matthew 5:13–16, Christ continues with His sermon: "You are the salt of the earth. However, if the salt loses its taste, with what can it be seasoned? It is no longer good for anything but to be thrown out and trampled underfoot. You are the light of the world. A city set on a mountain cannot be hidden. Nor do they light a lamp and then put it under a bushel basket; it is set on a lampstand, where it gives light to all in the house. Just so, your light must shine before others, that they may see your good deeds and glorify your heavenly Father." So beautiful, at this moment I had to practice what I believe, right? Belief is nothing without action. Christ here gave action to my belief. To show the world the conviction in what I believe. So, when someone sees me, I want them to say, "I do believe that his beliefs direct him."

## The Church of the Holy Sepulchre

We finished our time in Israel back in Jerusalem. There was one church we had not visited yet, the Church of the Holy Sepulchre, which stands on the site where Jesus was crucified. This was the church that was built upon the ground where Christ died for our sins.

We started at the beginning of the trail, the Via Dolorosa (the trail of the crucifixion), on which we would experience the full passion of Christ from beginning to end. We started at the Church of the Agony, which was where Christ prayed all night before His crucifixion. We arrived, read the related scripture passage, and prayed. Christ's disciples did not stay up to pray with Him, but my dad wanted to make sure that we did pray with the Lord. I like what my dad said during our prayer: He asked the Lord to prepare us to carry our crosses once we get back home.

We left the Church of Agony and began our journey to the Church of the Holy Sepulchre. We began at the beginning of the trail, where Jesus was whipped. Throughout this time, my dad had told us to pray quietly. I thought about the comment my dad had said earlier about carrying my cross. I realized that we all endure our own passion experience, just as Christ experienced His. We made our way down the Via Dolorosa and I prayed and prepared myself for the final site.

When we arrived at the Church of the Holy Sepulchre, I roamed throughout the whole church. This one was huge. It had two sides; the side where the cross stood and the side where Christ was laid. The side where Christ laid had a miniature church around a dome, you'd walk in through one side and out the other, the ground was very sacred and small with the miniature church. On the other side you had set of lamps around an altar, at the center of the alter you had Christ on the cross, below the alter there was glass and through the class you can see the crack, once Christ died there was a massive earthquake that made a crack on solid rock where Christ was crucified. I was quiet the whole time, staying in a state of prayer. Finally, I stood right in front of the cross and, at His feet, I kneeled and asked for forgiveness. I now had the resolve that I would carry my cross for the rest of my life.

The cross is our mission in life. Everybody has a mission, and mine is different from yours. We all go through things in life that will bring us down. Christ fell three times while carrying His cross. So, I realize it was ok to fail, but the most important thing was to get back up with the conviction of victory. Here, I realized that's what got Christ through. His passion was his belief in the mission to save humanity.

Christ's incredible true story is unmatched and authentic. But what makes it all so incredible is rooted in all life, if you are a believer of Christ or not, no matter the principle, no matter the system. A belief is something in all of us, but it has to be a far greater purpose than ourselves. The message is not to push you to believe in what I believe in but to awaken the purpose rooted in all of us which is gratitude, love and service. Christ represents that there is no greater glory than to die for what you believe in. In all of us there lies a truth to believe in gratitude, love and service and I believe that truth will prevail in the form of peace if we do this. There in Israel is where I found my belief in my incredible true story.

# Chapter 11: Love

*"Love recognizes no barriers. It jumps hurdles, leaps fences, penetrates walls, to arrive at its destination full of hope."*

*—Maya Angelou*

In my story, I found another purpose rooted in all humans: Love. Much like storytelling, love is in everything we do. In our everyday lives, in the people we decide to marry, become friends with, siblings, family, work, hobbies, sleep, eating, in literally everything. It is what positively moves the world; it is what allows us to live with each other. It allows us to experience moments differently or uniquely. Love lives within our belief, our why, our day to day experiences, and in others. It is what allows us to enjoy this life we live. But there is a much greater purpose to love. With love we need to take a much greater responsibility. Love is nothing without responsibility.

The love within my incredible true story makes it so much more unique. To tell you how I found the one thing that all human people pursue. Love is the one thing all human beings can't live without. To honestly tell your love and how you found it and to encourage others to do the same, well, that gives people hope. That gives people the ability to look for the good in tomorrow. That gives people the impact of being present in every moment. To truly build relationships that last. To build friendships that will collectively change you and the world. To tell you about the love of what you do in life. To tell you about the love of your significant other. To tell the love of life. We see here that with love we find a purpose far greater than living.

Like I said before, I witnessed love several times in my story, but the one time that I can remember vividly was in the beautiful city of Barcelona. That day in Barcelona, I witnessed love in two ways: Through work and through my parents.

# Barcelona

We arrived at our final destination in Spain: Barcelona. Our plane was to leave the following morning to take us to Israel. We arrived that afternoon, parked the car, and went to explore the city. Our first stop was the Sagrada Familia, the basilica that is still in the process of being built. It has been like that for decades. From the outside, the church was beautiful. When I asked who designed the building, the guide answered, "Antoni Gaudi."

Gaudi was a master in his craft. It is very hard to describe his work, it is very unique to the eye and it aligns with natures beauty. As a person, Gaudi was different. One of the reasons I love the city of Barcelona so much is because he made it so beautiful. Antoni Gaudi revolutionized architecture and many of the designs and works he spread throughout Barcelona are breathtaking. Gaudi was an innovator, a guy who took his work to the extra degree. Antoni Gaudi was iconic I found that Gaudi fell in love with what he did. His passion for art and nature made him an innovator in his field. He lived every day with the joy of art. That's why Barcelona is so beautiful.

Many of the tourist areas in Barcelona we visited were comprised of his works, but eventually, we ended up going into an area that makes Barcelona such a unique cultural treasure trove: Las Ramblas! Las Ramblas is a long street filled with stores and people. This was a place where gatherings and celebrations took place. Many people went there to hang out and show appreciation to each other. It was a very cool place to be, and I was having a wonderful time there. We followed the street until its end, and we eventually made it to the statue of Columbus that had been erected there. This small memorial had Columbus pointing out to the sea, signifying the beginning of the expedition.

Night came, and we walked along the Port of Barcelona. While we were walking, my mom asked my dad if he remembered that area. Then she laughed and said, "Of course you don't." My dad was confused, and then he said, "What do you mean?" My mom told us the story of the time they went to Europe together and came to Barcelona.

"It was our last few days in Europe, and your dad asked me to a fancy dinner at a high-end restaurant here in the city. We asked around, and they pointed us to this restaurant down the street from here. We had a great time with each other, we talked about our times as youths and the choices we made growing up and of course, we spoke about our kids. Throughout the night, your dad was drinking so much wine. He went through several bottles. He was so open to me for the first time; he kept repeating to me how much he loved me."

What I remember the most about my mom's story is how my dad had told her he was so in love with her. He went on and on, saying so many beautiful things to her, and he ended by saying that the best decision he had ever made was to choose her. We stood there, listening to the story, and my dad was so embarrassed that he was blushing. However, they had a moment right there again: They looked each other in the eye with so much belief, so much conviction, and so much love. I had never felt so much power in their relationship. My dad then repeated it: "I love you," and we all felt their everlasting bond. I stood there, feeling the passion and commitment of their love reaching me. It felt warm, healthy, and sincere.

Later, I pictured that story over and over in my head, but all I could see was love. It was like my parents had somehow transferred it to me. That was probably the happiest moment of my life; I was living a dream. At one point, it had all been a dream in my dad's head, but through his love, he made all of it a reality—a reality I will cherish forever. At that moment, I realized that love is living, made up of belief and so much sacrifice.

I realized that love is real, and I believe in it. At that moment, I never knew how powerful three words could be: "I love you." In conclusion, I came down to find that rooted in us all is the purpose for love. We are subjects of love, made out of love to love. Which brings us to a greater understanding that there is a greater responsibility that we must take up. Seeing my dad say those words to my mom gave me hope that humanity could one day take up this responsibility and find its way back to its real source of living: which ultimately is to love.

# Chapter 12: Mindset

*"Never say never because limits, like fears, are often just an illusion."*

*—Michael Jordan*

Through my incredible true story, I figured out things I needed to do to stay grounded and progress myself. I learned that a person always needs a healthy mindset to progress. What do I mean by this? If you recall my dad's story earlier in the book, I talk about how he was poor and had no support. One would think his mindset would be pessimistic. However, his mindset was strong, grounded, and fierce. It all began with this mindset, the idea that "yes I can" and the belief that the only person who could stop him was himself.

My dad has a strong mindset because of the way he grew up. He replicated the way he grew up and applied it to his kids. I have always said my dad was my first hater; if I could take negative criticism from him, then the critics of the world would be nothing to me. For the longest I always wanted to impress my dad, to show him that I was good enough, to finally hear an 'atta boy' or "I'm proud," but never did I get that. I never understood why until I realized what my dad wanted me to see. A mindset isn't about having a hard head when it comes to criticism. It's about knowing why you are doing something and that allows you to have a strong, grounded, and fierce mindset. Furthermore, knowing why you do something brings about purpose to your life and once you take responsibility for it there is no limit to what you can do.

For the longest, I was doing things to prove it to my dad that I was worth it, so in a sense, I was doing everything for him. I realized that I should be doing the things that will make me happy because I want to do them, not because I want to prove to others that I can or to be celebrated. A strong mindset is dependent on the reason you are doing something and if it will fulfill you. Once you start answering those questions, I honestly believe you can do anything you set your mind to.

# London

It was raining on our third day in London. It rained every day we were there, but we realized it always rains in London. We made our way around all of the city. It felt unreal, walking through the London Bridge, seeing Big Ben and Buckingham Palace. I kept thinking to myself how I had only seen these places in movies and books, now I was there. It all was amazing, but even that couldn't prevent a family fight.

We were walking along the roads of London, and my brothers started making comments about our future success in life and what we will all achieve. We all boasted and challenged what we were going to do in life. My dad overheard us and just laughed to himself a bit. Not to make fun of us but as if to say, "you haven't done anything yet, so stop talking." I was a bit offended. During that time, I was praised by many people. I was called a top leader, future president, and so many other things. I remember coming to my dad and telling him how much praise I had from people, but my dad scoffed it off and told me he didn't see much in me. He said at best I would become a McDonald's manager. At first, I was angry. I was burning up. I thought to myself, *How could he?* I was heating up! I was ready to go off, but then it hit me. *Why was I getting mad?* He was right. I hadn't done anything with my life, why am I showing off? Compliments are compliments; you can't take them literally. So, I thought, why did the compliments give me the right to boast? After that moment, I began thinking about how I thought and why I was doing these things. I told myself, *if I had a strong mindset, then I wouldn't be questioning myself.*

London was just the first stop of my month-long trip; after that moment, the rest of the trip changed for me.

# Chapter 13: Community

*"I'm a reflection of the community."*

*—Tupac Shakur*

My incredible true story led me to see what it means to be a community. I was also able to see what my community and other communities are lacking. I witnessed in this journey that real change happens within a community. There are layers to a community. First, the community of the home, then the community of the city, to the state, then the country and eventually the world. I witness the effects of what my home (the U.S.) had on the world and what the world had on my home.

My incredible true story also affected my outlook and impact on life. I not only visited communities across the world, but I visited historical grounds — the history of the lands and the fall of empires. This brought me to reflect more than just my life. I learned about how communities had fallen and how communities turned on each other. I had my eyes opened in several ways, ways that I couldn't imagine. I thought about my home, my community, and how much impact I was doing. I thought about the needs of my community. Then it hit me, what good is our freedom if we do not use it for good? Within the responsibilities rooted in all humans, there are two that we must put in our center threshold which are love and freedom. Realizing this, it gave me an urge to go home and be a part of my community, to make a positive change in our world.

This part of my incredible true story allowed me to see how small the world is and how big of an impact I can make.

# World War II

In my three trips to Europe and my two to Israel, I visited Auschwitz, Birkenau, the Warsaw Ghetto, the Krakow Ghetto, and the Israeli World War II Museum. I had many different feelings during my time there. I never really enjoyed my visits because I always felt death in those places. I call the grounds of Auschwitz "the devil's home" and the biggest cemetery in the world. It was a place where hate resided, where death was the odor, and where sadness was the mood. The stories I heard, the videos I watched, the books I read—all gave accurate descriptions of those places. The actions performed in those places were not human. They were barbaric. Only savages would have done things like that. I wasn't aware that I knew it was humans who did these things because I couldn't acknowledge the idea that the human race, God's greatest and most loved creation, could do such horrible things. We were so far from perfect—and we still are.

My time at Auschwitz was the most memorable because I had the experience of being there several different times. I walked in with a clear mind and a long period of silence. I knew the place I was in wasn't a place to socialize or take pictures. It was a place to be serious and to understand. Walking through the buildings, I began to see different pictures and descriptions of what had happened in individual rooms and locations on the campgrounds. All I saw was slaughter.

We walked into a block where the spirit felt different to me. In that block was the cell of Saint Maximilian Kolbe. It felt holy. I had never believed that in a place so full of darkness, there could be any light. Saint Maximilian was a Polish priest during the time of World War II. He was in Japan doing mission work, but after he heard the horror of what was occurring in his homeland, he went back home to help. In the process, he was captured by the Nazis and sent to Auschwitz. During one of his nights there, a few prisoners tried to escape but failed. The next morning, there was a random selection for the punishment for this crime. A man was chosen, but this man begged the Nazi soldiers to let him live, pleading that he had a wife and a child, but they refused. Saint Maximilian overheard and offered to take his place—and the Nazis agreed. They lined up those who were chosen in the courtyard, stripped them naked, and made them stand still in the cold with no food. If they moved, they were killed. The other choice for them was to move and then die because they had no food and water. Days went by, and the people start falling, one after another, but Saint Maximilian was still standing. Weeks went by, and eventually, he was the only one still standing. The Nazi soldiers, in shock, decided to poison him, which finally led to his death. The man he had saved, though, survived to tell the story.

My mom always told us that story, and my younger brother, Max, was named after this saint. In his cell and all of the other cells, there were carvings of Jesus Christ on the walls. In this time of darkness, many found the light of Christ. To many, that was their salvation, their impetus to survive, and to others that was their salvation when they died. While walking through the camp, I thought about all of the discrimination that was practiced against Jews, Christians, Catholics, homosexuals, those with special needs, and the disabled. I thought about the poverty they experienced, the homelessness they went through, the nakedness they endured, the thirst they felt, and the imprisonment that was forced upon them—for no reason.

Then I witnessed the gas chambers and crematoriums, and I broke. I could not believe it: They were real. At that moment, I wondered how cruel a human being could be. I hated that fact. These camps were communities of hell. They were grounds of the destruction of human beings—not just physically, but mentally. After I saw these buildings of death, I wanted to leave. I couldn't be there anymore.

After we finally left, my dad asked me, "What are you doing?" I didn't know what he meant. He asked again: "What are you doing?" He saw my confusion, and he continued, "The problems that arose in World War II are still happening. What are you doing to stop them? These are your real problems. These are the problems you should be worrying about. You know how worried you get when you lose your phone, or when you have homework that is due the next day but should have been completed the day it was assigned? Or when a girl breaks up with you, and you think it's the end of the world? Well, those aren't problems, they don't come near to what the real problems are. What are you doing to help your community back at home? What are you doing to make a difference? These are the questions that all humans should be worrying about, but now it is up to you to decide what you will do. Will you sit and hide cowardly behind everyone else, or will you act to change the world?"

I was still. I realized all the time that I had wasted, all the time that I could have been working for others. Literally right after my dad spoke those words, my mom read me these Bible verses from the book of Matthew: "For I was hungry, and you gave me food, I was thirsty, and you gave me something to drink, I was a stranger, and you welcomed me, I was naked, and you gave me clothing, I was sick, and you took care of me, I was in prison and you visited me" (25:35–37). I realized that I wasn't doing anything of worth and that I had to make a change in my life.

When we live with no greater purpose, then we have no responsibility. Which then makes you realize that you are doing nothing with your freedom. I realize that I have been given much and that I have a purpose and responsibility to use my freedom to give much more back. If all of those who are born with such privilege and opportunity and do nothing with it, then you have truly lost the true purpose for freedom. Reflecting on the sins that were spread from World War 2, The Red Terror and many uglier human events I saw that we did not take responsibility for our freedom and love. When we find that our own personal pleasures, emotions and wants are the purpose for our freedoms then we truly do die. How could I continue to live if there is still so much sin in this world? How could I continue to put my own selfish wants above the good I should be doing? How could I be so irresponsible with my freedom and love.

However, the biggest realization I made was that I was big in this world. The world isn't big, it's small. It only takes one person to cause a ripple effect of change. It's not governments or systems that make a change, it's the person that does. I came to a resolve that I am going to take responsibility for my freedom and love to do good in this world.

# Chapter 14: Leadership

*"A leader's job is not to do the work, it's to help others figure out how to do it themselves, to get things done, and to succeed beyond what they thought possible."*

*—Simon Sinek*

In my incredible true story, I figured out what I want to do in life. I found out it was leadership. During this part of my journey, I was fighting the urge to be a leader. In my heart, I knew I wanted to take those leadership roles at school and in my community to make a positive change. I wanted every bit of it, but I was afraid. I was afraid of the responsibility, of failing. So, I ran. I ran from that calling, that mission in life. However, it was only a matter of time until it caught back up to me.

In this part of my journey, I figured out that leadership isn't about having all the answers, changing the world, or making a substantial impact on something. It's about knowing that you don't have all the answers, that you might fail, and you might not make an impact. It's about knowing all those things and still doing it. It's about taking that risk of failure for the sake of seeking success. I figured out during this trip that I was called to lead.

This part of the journey explains a bit about how I was looking at leadership. However, by the end, I figured out that everyone has their script, their journey, their incredible true story, and my role as a leader, well, it would eventually find me, and I would find it. I just needed to take the risk.

# Italy

In my life, my two most significant role models in leadership were my parents. My dad led by example, and my mom led through teaching. I always say that my dad taught me how to work and my mom taught me how to love. But the greatest lesson learn from them is that I need to take responsibility for my life and purpose and to use my gifts for a greater good.

Growing up my mom always put the example of the Saints of the Catholic church to be a sort of representation of people who tried to emulate their life's based of Jesus Christ. However, The Catholic Church advises its members to select a saint, someone who has been revered by the Church and who showed authentic leadership within the Church, so while we go through life, we can try to model some of their characteristics. Before I made my final selection before my confirmation, I had chosen two different saints. These saints were Saint John Bosco of Turin, Italy, and Saint Francis of Assisi, Italy. Saint John Bosco had gotten involved with the male youth in Turin, where he was able to create a school for boys to learn to read, write, and pray. He would also give them a place to stay, feed them, and offer them work. Now there are lodges and schools like this all over the world, which not only help all sorts of people. I loved the story of John Bosco, but I never felt an actual connection with him, and we are encouraged to find a saint with whom we can connect in a way where we are similar in characteristics. John Bosco wasn't the saint for me. However, I still ended up taking a lot of what his story taught me and getting involved in my community based on his teachings.

I began to read up on other saints, and when I stumbled across Saint Francis of Assisi, I read that he was a spoiled child when he was growing up. After he got older, he wanted to go to war in the Crusades, but he wasn't physically or mentally equipped for it. He didn't last long as a soldier, but he was embarrassed to return home. One day he decided to go to Church and pray about his future. During his time of prayer, it is said that the large crucifix on the wall came to life and told Saint Francis to go and "rebuild My Church."

There was a church down the street from where Francis lived that was abandoned and destroyed, and he thought that Christ meant that he should physically rebuild that Church. As such, Francis rebuilt the Church down the street from his home.

One day in that remodeled church, he was sitting and praying when the crucifix came alive again and said the same thing: "Go and rebuild My Church." Francis finally realized that Christ was calling him to go and rebuild His universal church. At the time, the Catholic Church was in a bad state. Saint Francis created the Franciscan Order, which to this day is still at work helping the poor and the sick. When Francis created this order, he positively reformed the Church. I thought the story was cool, but again, I had no actual connection with it.

Now our final stop in Italy was Rome. Rome has always been special to our family; we love it so much. Rome is so much more special to me, because underneath the Vatican Saint Pope John Paul the Great body resides. I have a connection to Saint John Paul the Great. He was the saint I selected for my confirmation. A few years before the trip Pope Benedict XVI canonize John Paul as a saint in the Catholic Church. It was probably the most important news the Catholic Church had received in years. My family was ecstatic. It was great news. At the time, I knew enough about him to know that he was one of the greatest popes in the history of the Catholic

Church. I had visited and seen the places where he used to live, teach, and go to school. I visited the place where he became a priest, where he gave mass. I knew all about his life before he was pope. I was so fascinated by his life story.

One day we were praying as a family, and we had his picture resting on the podium where we also have our statue of Christ and our Holy Bible. During our prayer, something or someone was calling me toward the picture. It was like Pope John Paul II was telling me to pick him. It was screaming in my heart to choose him as my saint. It suddenly felt like we were the perfect match, and I was caught in awe for a while. After we were through praying, I went to look in the tub where my mom kept all our childhood pictures. There I saw the pictures of my baptism. I was dressed up like Pope John Paul II—my clothes were baby garments of his clothes. My baptism pictures were the sign to me that I had a connection to Pope John Paul II. My confirmation was where I accepted my religion as a full human who could think and reason for myself. It was only right that I should pick Pope John Paul II to continue with my religious life. So I did— I selected him. It wasn't until my trip to Italy that I accepted my vocation as a leader.

Italy was the final country in our third month long world tour as a family. Our first stop in Italy was Turin, where we were going to visit the memorial Church of Saint John Bosco. Crazy how that was our first stop. I recall my mom telling me to apologize to him for not picking him to be my saint for confirmation. I laughed it off, but I was thinking about the idea of what a saint meant in my life. At this time, I was battling the fact that I did not want to be a leader, but everyone was telling me that I was. Every time I prayed for guidance from God, all I got were signs about leadership. I walked into the church and said a little prayer. I sat next to my mom, and she said to me, "Why haven't you answered God's call?" I sat there in silence. She then said, "Father Rusty wants you to get involved with the youth group and help the teens in the community. Pray to Saint John Bosco so he can give you the guidance of the Lord."

I sat there still in silence, but I wondered how ironic it was that my mom would tell me that our parish priest wanted me to get involved in the church community. I felt the presence of God there, and I felt that leadership was my true calling, but I was too scared to answer the call at that time. How much was I going to leave behind to take up my cross? I had been running from this responsibility for my whole life at that moment. I stood firm in my faith and accepted my calling. I knew that was Saint John Bosco's gift for me, the push I needed before I left to start my journey because it all began with him. He awakened my love for leadership.

A few days later, we made our way to Assisi, Italy. You know, by that time, I was starting to think that God was not going to accept my denial of being a leader. We arrived late to Assisi, so we didn't go to the Church until the next day. I didn't think of anything that night. We entered the Church the next day, and I was just amazed. The main church was set on top of the mountain of Assisi, and the view was beautiful. I walked in the church and took a seat with my mom, and she then told me Father Rusty (the parish priest) was going to send me to a retreat called LEAD. This retreat was hosted by the Franciscan University in Steubenville, Ohio. If you remember, I said that Saint Francis of Assisi had founded the Franciscan order. Well, this university had been built by the Franciscan order. So, to put it in perspective, I was being told that I was going to a retreat known as LEAD that would help me with my leadership and faith life, and the people who were sponsoring it and leading it were from the Franciscan University—and I was told this at the Church of Saint Francis of Assisi, in Assisi, Italy. At that moment of realization, there was no more running. It was time for me to grow up and take up my cross of leadership. I knew where this all should adequately begin, and I knew where I had to go next: Rome.

Within the Vatican, there is a big room where they keep every pope's coffin. Pope John Paul II's coffin was there, and I knew I had to make my way there because my cross was waiting there for me to pick up. We got to Rome, where we rented an apartment for three days across from the Vatican. We made our way over to the Vatican the next day. I made it a mission to go and see the tomb of the Popes. I didn't care how long I had to wait—I was willing to fight for it. I eventually made my way down to John Paul II's tomb, where I stood and said a silent prayer.

Later that day, I reflected on the stories of those saints, and how their mission in life found them and they found it. I realized it was all coming together, that it was coming to me. These stories, there connection to the church and their impact on the world where all part of their mission. The conclusion and what my parents tried to tell me is that these people lived their life doing their best to emulate Jesus Christ, within this challenge they found three purposes: gratitude, service and love. Within those purpose and the freedom, they possess, they took responsibility for their purposes which enable their true life calling to present itself. The conclusion that I am making is that we all have the purpose of gratitude, service and love and we possess the freedom to choose to take responsibility for it. My mission in life was finding me during this period. Now the next step was for me to go out and accept it. I chose to take the risk and begin my mission of leadership.

My question to you is, will you take the risk in choosing to be grateful, be of service and to love others?

# Chapter 15: World

*"Enjoyment of the landscape is a thrill."*

*—David Hockney*

Throughout my first trip, I realized how much I was learning, but one thing I didn't do was enjoy it. It wasn't because I didn't want to, I was learning so much and thinking about what I was going to do when I get back home and I wasn't present. In my incredible true story, one valuable lesson I learned is to always be present in everything you do.

The first trip was so overwhelming because I saw so much and took so much in. After the second and third trip, I decided to go into these places and be present, to really enjoy the moment and take it all in. I decided to apply that to my everyday life, whenever I am with family, friends, class, or at work, to stay present in the moment. That's how you live and enjoy life. You can't appreciate life until you enjoy what you have at the moment.

I always found myself very out of the moment because I would be thinking about work, grades, or something other than the moment. That ruined the present for me; it gave me reasons not to go out, not to be social. I decided to adjust and start being in the moment. It made my daily life more enjoyable and less stressful. At the end of every day, I think about my day and put it in perspective, I think of the new ideas I heard, the people I met, how I used my time and whether or not I set out to do what I wanted.

I learned that the enjoyment of the moment can make you happy in ways you never thought possible. Your incredible true story is you living in the moment – being there, enjoying the moment and most importantly, learning. You can't tell your incredible true story until you start living in the moment because that's when you start to fully understand your incredible true story.

# The Pyramids of Giza

I remember reading in my seventh-grade geography textbook about Egypt. We learned about ancient Egypt, and going through the pages of the book, I would see the different parts of Egypt. Then we got to the most important part: The Pyramids. Never in a thousand years did I ever think that within a few months I would be standing in front of that magnificent image.

We were heading out to Giza, ready to go. I was so excited that I was about to witness such historical greatness in person. I was going to see the three great pyramids of Giza and the Sphinx. In my mind, I was passing through a time machine. I knew that all of Egypt was already special, but I was going to see the cherry on the top. I was going to witness what really made Egypt, *Egypt*. How could I be so lucky?

The opportunity finally arrived, and I stood in front of the gate that led onto the grounds of the Pyramids. I saw over the walls the tip of the greatness. I finally got in and was able to see past the wall. I entered a world of imagination. I went back in time as an Egyptian ruler, and I stood there seeing the Pyramids being built. I came back to life, and walking through it all I stumbled upon a young man who offered us camels to ride while we toured the Pyramids. We got on, and I felt like I truly was Indiana Jones. I was the explorer traveling through the lands of the desert, looking for ancient artifacts, and collecting data. In that process, I embarked on a crazy adventure. I was lost for words. I went alongside one of the three Pyramids, and I felt like an ant. The size difference was glorious. It was hard climbing the Pyramids because the boulders were so big. After circling the perimeter several times, I finally stood up and saw the view. I embraced it, knowing that I might not ever get to see an image so amazing and glorious ever again. I thought to myself, *How? What technology? What skills? What ability?* And then I asked, *Why? Why did God give us such beautiful things as this?* As I stood there, I realized that the world is made up of so much more than objects and ideas. It is made up of art and beliefs, it is driven by nature within the seasons, it changes and transforms into beauty. There are things that, as humans, we can never understand—and that's okay—but what we should know is that humanity was formed through nature and art. Antoni Gaudi said it himself: "Anything created by human beings is already in the great book of nature." He also said, "Those who look for the laws of nature as a support for their new works collaborate with the creator."

What man creates becomes nature, and nature in turn collaborates with the Creator. I stood in front of God's work and to this day I believe that as humans we lack the art of nature, and as humans we lack in collaboration with our Creator.

# Granada

We woke up in the city of Granada, Spain, a beautiful city in the high country of La Piel del Toro. We were so excited for the day ahead, for on top of the city there stood a magnificent castle. It made the city look way more special than most of the other cities we visited. Our mission was to climb to the top, to the highest point, and to see the world from there. We started walking away from our hotel, we pushed up and eventually arrived at the foot of the castle. Right when I passed the gate, I felt like a Spanish conquistador. I was making my way up to see the king and queen. After traversing the long roads and the massive stairs, I reached the first point of the castle—a courtyard. It was fascinating. I saw many school kids in the courtyard, and it seemed like the students were on a field trip.

I could see a good part of the city from the courtyard, and my dad thought that was the peak of our voyage, but I knew there was more. I searched the whole courtyard until I found another part of the castle that we could access. We began to walk through the rooms and the central courtyards of the castle. The designs of the castle were so beautiful; the marble and colors intertwined, and you could notice that the architecture wasn't Spanish. My dad started to explain that it was Arabic architecture. Back when the Ottoman Empire tried to conquer Spain, they went through parts of the city and started changing the architecture in many places. The castles were covered in these designs, and they made the castles look beyond amazing.

I began to slow down and started embracing where I was. I was beginning to enter the peak of the castle, but I didn't stop to notice where I had been. I stopped in the middle of the castle and just started looking around. I thought to myself that I was no longer in Oklahoma. I was in a whole other part of the world. I started thinking more about the Spanish Empire. Then I started to think about history in general. I thought about all the places I had seen before our trip to Granada. While I was thinking, I made my way up the stairs to the peak of the castle.

I closed my eyes before I got to the top. Then I stopped, inhaled a deep breath, and opened my eyes, to see the magnificent image of God. I was at a peak, and I felt powerful. I stood at the top, and I felt like the ruler of the world. Being up there, I closed my eyes, and the wind blew and pressed against my face. I felt like I was flying. I was free, free of all responsibility, free of all work, and free of everyone else. I was alone with God. I was so amazed to see what the world could offer a person. I became wealthy up on that peak—not rich in money, but rich in my embrace of the landscape. I embraced every single aspect of the land: the buildings, the trees, and the people. I embraced it all and found peace on that peak.

I've begun to notice how the world is so focused on the small screen on our phones. Walking around in my daily life, all I see is people staring at their phones, to the point that they can't look up and see the landscape of life. They can't let go of technology to get outside and embrace the beauty of the world. They can't embrace the overall landscape of life. We begin to lose real value in the crucial things in life like personal connection when this happens. Relationships are what move this world. They are what drive human beings. There are several times when I have sat with my friends in silence and enjoyed the landscape of life with them. I sit there and see them and think: this is my family. I think about our futures with our families and how our kids will become best friends with each other. I truly embrace the landscape of life.

Don't lose yourself within the screen, look up and embrace the landscape of life and be at peace within yourself.

# Rome

Rome shares a special place in my heart. It is one of my greatest loves. It is very mythical, ancient, and modern, all at once. As a family, we always made a tradition to always end our trips in Rome. This place began the most considerable change in my life. What do I mean by this? Rome was the first place I visited when I went overseas for the first time.

Rome has had this influence on me from the get-go. The way the streets are set up is so different from everything else; they have this great appeal to them. Walking through the city was an experience, and just seeing the ruins all over the city was spontaneous. You could be walking down the street, surrounded by the best of what technology has to offer, and then you can turn and see the ancient ruins right there within the city. The city itself is very magical; it can make you fall in love. I always said that if I ever take my future wife anywhere, it would be to Italy, because that is where I fell in love. Going through the city, seeing all the beautiful churches built for glory and gold captivated my eyes. Every church, all the way to the Vatican, has made me speechless to the core. Castel Sant'Angelo was gorgeous and fabulous at the same time. I felt like a ruler visiting each of these places.

Going into the Sistine Chapel was also mind-opening. The art and architecture—all were glorious to the mind. Don't get me started with the old Roman monuments. The colosseum was notorious, the Roman Forum, the Pantheon, the Trevi Fountain, and the Arc of Titus—all opened me up to a world beyond my own life. The architecture, the food, the art, and the culture—all took me to another level of life.

Rome was the place that began my initial growth in wanting to see more of the world. After our visit to Rome, I felt like I was wasting my life in Oklahoma in a way where I wasn't maximizing my life in Oklahoma. That trip was the greatest mind opener. I wanted to experience more of life, knowledge, and culture. I wanted to conquer the world. I wanted to learn everything. I wanted to know it all, but I also wanted to see the beauty of the world. The world offers us the most significant things in our lives, but it is all focused-on parts of what planet earth is. The greatest gifts live within every land. When you're not seeing the world and not seeing the true beauty of what it offers, you are not truly living. The world creates, but it can never destroy. Go and see the creation of life.

Feel it, embrace it, absorb it, and give it back to the world. The only way we grow as a people is to give back our knowledge of the world. That's why we study geography, history, and other subjects of the world. English, math, politics, and religion—literally everything has been given to us by the world and it was given to us from all parts of the world. The world is the fruit and we must bite into this fruit, but we cannot finish the fruit only to throw it to waste on the floor. God wanted us to learn about life through the rare earth He gave to us.

# Chapter 16: Why

*"He who has a why to live can bear almost any how."*

*— Friedrich Nietzsche*

At the end of my last trip, the final lesson I learned and the key to every Incredible True Story is to have a *why*. A *why* in life is the one question that will carry you through it all. A 'why' isn't just a question, but it's your power, what makes you unique, it's everything about you. I started with my 'why,' because I wanted you to know why I wrote this, but I also ended with my 'why' because learning it was the outcome of my trips.

A person's 'why' is the most significant thing in their life. The world continues to move because of people's 'why' in life. It is the 'why' in life that opens the world to new heights, new journeys, new worlds, and new challenges. It is the 'why' in life that connects people. It calls for reason and understanding. It opens the mind and helps you think. Your 'why' will always be the one thing that makes you different. At the end of it all, remember that you always have a choice in this life, a choice to decide what you want to do and who you want to be. Your 'why' will affect that. As you see in my parents' story, they chose the life they wanted, and they were motivated by their 'why'. You have the choice to your life, you always have.

Once I came home, I told myself that I couldn't go back to my regular life; there was just no way of doing so. I chose to pursue what my heart and soul were calling me to do. I found my 'why,' and I made sure my 'why' was more significant than the world I saw, I made sure my 'why' was more important than any selfish ideas, and I made sure that it was going to be my 'why' that would take me out of this universe.

From when I started writing this book my junior year of high school to finally coming to life, the manuscript changed about five times. A bit like life, the purpose of the book changed. When I revisited these stories and sat with my family to put the words that created this book, I reflected on my life. I wrote down the most significant experiences of my life up to that point, I then wrote all that I did good and learned from those experiences. I then wrote about my present life and all the good that I was doing. I finished with writing two futures, the future that I wanted for myself and the future that I did not want for myself. Once I crunch all of the experiences together, I notice that I was moving in the direction that I did not want.

The purpose of writing this book is not so you can agree with me or disagree with me, not to tell you about my views of life. I wrote this book with the sole purpose to express the three underlining themes of life. Which is Reflection: past, present and future. To know where you are going, you must know where you have been and where you are. Through this you are able to make experience into knowledge and knowledge into wisdom. Theme number two: Purpose. We as humans have three purposes rooted in us all. Which is gratitude, service and love. Once you understand what you have you will know that your next step is to serve others. To be of service in the time of need and anytime at all, because we are capable of serving and being served. Once you are living your purpose of gratitude and service the byproduct is love. The last theme is responsibility. Reflection, purpose, love and freedom are nothing without responsibility. As humans it is our duty to take up the responsibility of our freedoms to reflect, be purposeful and to love. Within doing these things you will know the true meaning of life.

After I came down with this conclusion, I made a deal with myself. The deal was when the day comes and I meet my Creator, that I can bring Him my life and show Him that I left it all on the line, that I gave all the love that I could, that I serve the world with all that I had, and that I rinsed every bit of talent, gift and resource that my Creator gave me. I decided that I want to live a life that I could be proud of and that is to love and serve. And when I stand before Him all I pray is that He will have mercy on my soul.

Now I sit here and write the words that ignited my Incredible True Story. The words that my parents spoke to me when I stood outside of Auschwitz, Poland. I write these words to you and say *What are you doing in life?* With that, I start your Incredible True Story. This is your platform, use it. You may never know; your Incredible True Story could lead to a great book or movie. Your Incredible True Story is built for you, make the best of it. I hope you enjoyed my Incredible True Story and hopefully, one day, I get to enjoy yours.